Cambridge Elements ≡

Elements in Psycholinguistics
edited by
Paul Warren
Victoria University of Wellington

STRUCTURAL PRIMING IN SENTENCE PRODUCTION

Giulia M. L. Bencini
University of Bologna

CAMBRIDGE
UNIVERSITY PRESS

Shaftesbury Road, Cambridge CB2 8EA, United Kingdom

One Liberty Plaza, 20th Floor, New York, NY 10006, USA

477 Williamstown Road, Port Melbourne, VIC 3207, Australia

314–321, 3rd Floor, Plot 3, Splendor Forum, Jasola District Centre,
New Delhi – 110025, India

103 Penang Road, #05–06/07, Visioncrest Commercial, Singapore 238467

Cambridge University Press is part of Cambridge University Press & Assessment,
a department of the University of Cambridge.

We share the University's mission to contribute to society through the pursuit of
education, learning and research at the highest international levels of excellence.

www.cambridge.org
Information on this title: www.cambridge.org/9781009478618

DOI: 10.1017/9781009236713

First published 2025

A catalogue record for this publication is available from the British Library

ISBN 978-1-009-47861-8 Hardback
ISBN 978-1-009-23669-0 Paperback
ISSN 2753-9768 (online)
ISSN 2753-975X (print)

Structural Priming in Sentence Production

Elements in Psycholinguistics

DOI: 10.1017/9781009236713
First published online: January 2025

Giulia M. L. Bencini
University of Bologna
Author for correspondence: Giulia M. L. Bencini, giulia.bencini@unibo.it

Abstract: This Element provides an overview of structural priming research across the three main populations on which experimental priming studies have concentrated: adult monolingual speakers, first language learners, and second language learners and bilinguals. Priming studies with monolingual adults were originally designed to inform psycholinguistic models of grammatical encoding in language production. Thanks to the implicit nature of the task, priming has turned out to be suitable for experimentally addressing questions about linguistic representation and use at the sentence level in speakers of any age. The view that priming is a form of implicit learning has sparked an interest in exploring continuity and life-long learning in language, opening up rich research areas in second-language acquisition and bilingualism. Priming rightly deserves to be a part of every language scientist's tool kit.

Keywords: structural priming, sentence production, structural priming in adults, structural priming in first language acquisition, structural priming in second language acquisition and bilingualism

ISBNs: 9781009478618 (HB), 9781009236690 (PB), 9781009236713 (OC)
ISSNs: 2753-9768 (online), 2753-975X (print)

Contents

1 Introduction

Structural priming has played a prominent role in advancing our understanding of the linguistic representations and processes involved when speakers turn their ideas into utterances they intend to produce. Specifically, it has greatly informed what we know of the stage in this process known as *grammatical encoding*, which is prior to any overt spoken, written, or signed output.

In structural priming studies, participants are presented with a prime sentence and then asked to produce a target sentence. Structural priming (also known as structural/syntactic persistence/adaptation) occurs when speakers, writers, or signers reuse the same structure as the prime. Structural priming was first studied experimentally by Kathryn Bock (1986b) in the spoken modality, and a large proportion of the structural priming literature deals with spoken production. Two influential studies have found structural priming in the written modality (Pickering & Branigan, 1998; Hartsuiker et al., 2008) with one study directly comparing priming in different modalities (Harstuiker et al., 2008). Structural priming has also been documented in a sign language (Hall, Ferreira, & Mayberry, 2015).

The structural priming paradigm developed by Bock (1986b) involves a sequence of events, with prime-target trials embedded in a long list of filler trials (see Figure 1). In this seminal study, a spoken priming sentence was presented in one of two structural alternatives. The study included two types of priming trials: active/passive prime sentences (1.1a and 1.1b) and prepositional object dative/double object dative prime sentences (1.2a and 1.2b). Following Bock (1986b) and subsequent priming literature, we will use the term *transitive trials* to refer to the (mono) transitive active/passive set, and *dative trials* to refer to the (di) transitive prepositional object dative/double object dative set. On target trials, participants were asked to describe pictures of events of the same type (transitive/dative) of the prime. For the transitive set, pictures depicted an action with two participants (e.g., lightning striking a church, a ball hitting a boy). For the dative set, pictures depicted an action with three participants (e.g., a boy handing a paintbrush to a girl). Prime sentences and target pictures were purposefully created so as to have different verbs or actions (e.g., *punch* in the prime, *strike* in the target) and different participants (e.g., *fans* and *referee* in the prime, *lightning* and *church* in the target). This was to reduce the probability that priming relied on lexical repetition, in order to isolate repetition of a more abstract kind, at the level of sentence structure. Throughout this Element, we will use the term *abstract priming* to refer to priming that does not depend on lexical repetition.

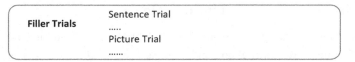

Filler Trials
  Sentence Trial
  .....
  Picture Trial
  ......

Priming Trial
Prime Sentence Trial
The woman was stung by the jellifish
[Participant Repeats]
Participant makes Recognition decision Yes/No

Target Picture Trial

Participant describes the picture
The boy is hit by a ball
Participant makes Recognition decision Yes/No

Filler Trials
  Picture Trial
  .....
  Sentence Trial
  ......

Figure 1 Experimental priming paradigm developed by Bock (1986b).

(1.1)   PRIMES
        a. One of the football fans punched the referee (ACTIVE)
        b. The referee was punched by one of the football fans (PASSIVE)

        TARGETS
        c. Lighting is striking a church (ACTIVE)
        d. The church is being struck by lightning (PASSIVE)

(1.2)   PRIMES
        a. A rockstar sold some cocaine to an undercover agent (PREPOSITIONAL
           OBJECT DATIVE)
        b. A rockstar sold an undercover agent some cocaine (DOUBLE OBJECT
           DATIVE)

        TARGETS
        c. The man is reading a story to the boy (PREPOSITIONAL OBJECT DATIVE)
        d. The man is reading the boy a story (DOUBLE OBJECT DATIVE)

Priming in Bock's study was embedded in a running recognition memory cover task with a long series of fillers – sentences and pictures – so participants were not aware of the real goal of the study. Fillers appeared more than once over the course of the experiment. Participants were told that their task was to decide whether they had encountered a sentence or picture before or during the experiment. They were also instructed to repeat each sentence out loud and to describe each picture, as an aid for the memory task. Hearing and repeating a prime sentence in the active such as 1.1a increased the likelihood of producing a target description using an active sentence (1.1c), whereas hearing and repeating a passive such as 1.1b increased the likelihood of producing a passive (1.1d). Similar effects were found for prepositional object (PO) datives and double object (DO) datives. A PO prime, as in 1.2a, made it more likely that speakers would produce a PO description as in 1.2c, and a DO prime, as in 1.2b, increased the likelihood of a DO target as in 1.2d.

Prior to being investigated experimentally, structural priming was first observed in naturalistic settings, both written and spoken (Estival, 1985; Levelt & Kelter, 1982; Tannen, 1989; Weiner & Labov, 1983). There is now a substantial body of carefully designed corpus-based priming research. Corpus priming research is extremely important as it not only provides evidence that converges with the experimental data but also demonstrates the ecological validity and generalizability of priming effects outside of experimental settings (Gries, 2005; 2011; for a review and dicussion, see Gries & Koostra, 2017). Our focus in this Element, however, is on experimental structural priming studies (Branigan 2007; Branigan & Pickering, 2017; Ferreira & Bock, 2006; Jackson, 2018; Kootstra & Myusken, 2017; Mahowald et al., 2016; Pickering & Ferreira, 2008; van Gompel & Arai, 2017).

The priming logic. The logic in structural priming experiments is simple yet powerful: if two stimuli are related along known dimensions and priming occurs, that is, one can detect the influence of the prime on the target, then we can conclude that the shared dimension is relevant to the representations engaged by the language system. If the shared dimension is unique (e.g., words, syntax, semantics, pragmatics, prosody) and priming is found, this supports the inference that the shared dimension is a cognitively isolable dimension during the processes of language production (Bock & Kroch, 1989). Structural priming can also be applied to adjudicate between different analysis of a linguistic phenomenon. If one account assumes that structures A and B are similar, but another account proposes that A and C are similar, priming between A and B and priming between A and C can be compared, relative to a baseline control structure D. If priming occurs between A and B relative to the baseline, but priming between A and C does not differ from the baseline, this can be taken as evidence in support of the analysis where A and B are represented and processed similarly. Like any negative result, failure to find priming must also be interpreted with caution as it could simply be that the manipulation was not sensitive enough to pick up the effect, or that different sources of priming cancel each other out. A positive effect must also be interpreted with reference to a representational theory and a language processing model, to pinpoint the locus of the effect.

Although priming was investigated in monolingual adults about fifteen years prior to being studied in children, second language learners, and multilinguals, the implicit nature of the priming task has turned out to be well-suited to address representational questions in a broader range of speakers, including young children for whom eliciting explicit metalinguistic judgments may not be appropriate. A common thread across the three populations is that priming can be used to probe into the nature of the sentence-level linguistic representations that are accessed during language use. Some of the representational questions addressed via priming are:

- What stages do adult native speakers go through when they produce utterances? Do adult speakers generate a sentence structure and then insert words into the structure, or do they first choose words and build the structure around those words?
- Are there stages in production during which structure is built independent of meaning?
- Are children's early sentences organized around specific words they hear used frequently in their input, or do children represent sentences with the same linguistic building blocks as adults?
- How do multilinguals represent syntactic information in their different languages? Do they keep their representations separate, or do they form language independent representations for structures that are similar across languages?

The rest of Section 1 provides the necessary psycholinguistic background, first introducing the reader to models of sentence production – and more specifically *grammatical encoding* – which were developed by psycholinguists to account for how monolingual adults produce language, where again, the research has mostly focused.

1.1 Models of Sentence Production

A psycholinguistic theory (or model) of sentence production makes explicit what happens in a speaker's mind when they turn a prelinguistic intention to communicate something into a linguistic expression that can be articulated as either spoken, written, or signed language. Sentence production is conceptually driven: speakers start out with a meaning (encoded in a preverbal message) and end up with a form (a phonological representation). At the same time, there is consensus among psycholinguists that production is not a shallow or direct mapping process from thinking to speaking: production proceeds through separable representational steps, corresponding broadly to the divisions between semantics, syntax, and phonology, whereby linguistic units of different kinds are selected, retrieved, and assembled online.

Since the seminal work of Garrett (1975), psycholinguists have worked within a consensus model of production with a two-stage architecture in which lexical semantic representations are retrieved independently of form-based, phonological representations (Bock, 1995; Bock & Ferreira, 2014; Bock and Levelt, 1994; Dell, 1986; Ferreira, Morgan, & Slevc, 2018; Ferreira & Slevc, 2007; Garrett, 1980a; 1980b; 1982; 1988; Levelt, 1989; Roelofs & Ferreira, 2019). Following Ferreira and colleagues (2018), we will call this the *two-stage consensus model for sentence production.*

To illustrate the main components of the consensus model, we will consider the grammatical encoding stages of a simple active English sentence (see Figure 2), suitable as a description of the transitive event of a "ball hitting a boy" (see Figure 3). One type of elicitation task used in sentence production studies, including structural priming studies, involves the use of pictures of events with two or three characters engaged in some kind of action, as in Figure 3. Participants are instructed to describe "what's happening in the picture" using one sentence. The combination of providing speakers with a picture and giving them instructions constrains the production task in important ways. First, pictures constrain

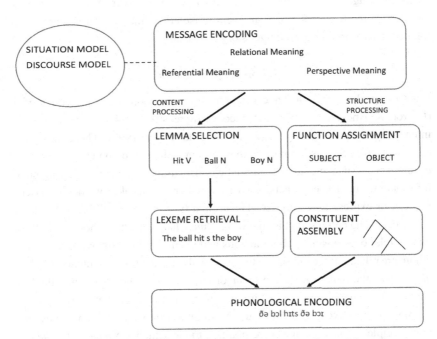

Figure 2 Grammatical encoding model for the generation of the sentence "The ball hit the boy."

Figure 3 Picture used to elicit a transitive sentence.

the types of ideas or messages speakers are likely to form. This is an important condition in priming studies, where the interest is mostly frequently in seeing what the effect of a prime sentence is on production, while controlling for aspects of the message. Second, the instruction to use one sentence also constrains speakers to focus on describing an event in isolation, and not, for example, use the image as a prompt for a longer story or narrative.

1.1.1 Message Encoding

Prior to speaking, people have a mental representation of a situation model (Garrod & Anderson, 1987) that encodes dimensions of reference, causality, intentionality, space, and time (Zwaan & Radvansky, 1998). These *messages* (Levelt, 1989) serve as input to grammatical encoding, and contain at least four different types of semantic and pragmatic information. The first type is pragmatic information about speech acts, such as whether the speaker wishes to assert, request, or express their surprise. The second type is referential meaning about participants and entities, that is "the who," "the what," and "the whom." The third type is relational meaning about actions and events, or how the who, what, and whom are related. For example, in the preverbal message for the sentence *The ball hit the boy*, the ball entity is the *hitter* or the AGENT of the action, and the boy entity is the one receiving the hitting action, the *hittee* or the PATIENT. Even a simple picture like the one in Figure 3 can give rise to more than one message. For example, in the message corresponding to the sentence *Someone hit the boy with a ball*, the unspecified human entity someone would be the *hitter* and AGENT, the ball would be the INSTRUMENT, and the boy would still be the *hittee* and PATIENT. The fourth type is discourse-pragmatic information. Speakers choose what information is more or less prominent, what information is in the background (given, old, or topical information) and what is in the foreground (focused, new, or comment) in a given context. Languages have systematic ways of encoding these distinctions, in a component of grammar referred to as information-structure (Lambrecht, 1994). The information that messages require may depend on the language the speaker is using. For example, languages vary with respect to whether a speaker must specify features such as definiteness, gender, number, animacy, tense, aspect, and so forth. Messages may therefore be viewed as a particular type of linguistic cognition – Slobin (1996) has aptly coined the expression "thinking for speaking" to refer to the constraints on packaging "thought for talk."

1.1.2 Grammatical Encoding

One major assumption in the consensus model is the separation of the processes that specify the content of an utterance from those that are responsible for its form. Structural priming studies have turned out to be very informative in addressing this question experimentally. Theoretically, the argument has also been made that an architecture that separates content and form is needed to capture a core feature of language, namely its expressive power (for a discussion, see Ferreira, Morgan, and Slevc, 2018). The consensus model of grammatical encoding also assumes that there is a distinction between so-called *functional processes* and *positional processes* (following Garrett, 1980a, see also Bock and Levelt, 1994). Functional processes are responsible for selecting abstract lexical representations or lexical entries (Bock, 1995) called *lemmas* (e.g., Kempen & Huijbers, 1983; Levelt, 1989; Roelofs, 1992; 1993) suitable for encoding the speaker's lexical meaning. Crucially, lemmas do not contain phonological information, which is instead "filled in" in a separate processing stage downstream from the grammatical encoding stage, called *phonological encoding*. During the phonological encoding stage, word forms (Garrett, 1975) or *lexemes* (Kempen & Huijbers, 1983; Levelt, 1989) are retrieved and assembled. To get an intuitive idea of the distinction between *lemma* representations and *lexeme* representations, it is useful to think of tip-of-the-tongue (TOT) states, when the speaker knows there is a word suitable to convey their intended meaning in the message (i.e., successful lemma access) but temporarily fails to access the phonological representation (i.e., unsuccessful lexeme retrieval). The output of phonological encoding is a phonetic plan (which is still part of inner speech) that serves as input to articulatory processing for overt speech production.

In earlier models of grammatical encoding, lemmas contained both lexical-semantic and lexical-syntactic information (e.g., Bock & Levelt, 1994). Later models (e.g., Levelt, Roelofs, & Meyer 1999; see Roelofs & Ferreira, 2019) restricted lemmas to specifying syntactic information, such as grammatical category (e.g., noun, verb, adjective, adverb) and grammatical features (e.g., grammatical gender, number, tense). In most of versions of the consensus model, lemmas are assumed to be abstract modality-general representations, shared between comprehension and production (Levelt et al. 1999; Roelofs, Meyer, & Levelt, 1998; see Ferreira et al., 2018). In addition to dealing with content information in the form of selecting lemmas, functional processing also deals with structural information, specifically the hierarchical relations required to compute grammatical dependencies (following Garrett, 1980a, we will use the descriptive notion *grammatical functions*, such as subject, direct object, indirect object). Following Garrett (1980a), an additional two-stage process is hypothesized: the functional level represents grammatical functions such as subject, direct object, or indirect object, but not linearized constituent order, which is instead specified at the later positional processing stage.

For our example active sentence used to describe the event in Figure 3, conceptually suitable lemmas to express the message behind the sentence *The ball hit the boy* are the nominal lemmas $[ball]_N$, $[boy]_N$ and the verb lemma $[hit]$ v. In the active English sentence in our example, functional processing selects the grammatical functions SUBJECT and DIRECT OBJECT, to which the selected lemmas are to be assigned: $[ball]_N$ to SUBJECT, and $[boy]_N$ to DIRECT OBJECT. The next component of grammatical encoding in the two-stage model is *positional processing*. This is where constituents are assembled into a linearized (but still abstract) sentence frame, with syntactically specified slots into which the selected lemmas are to be inserted. Positional encoding is also the stage during which functional elements (function words and grammatical endings) are specified. In our example, definite determiners and the past tense feature on the verb are specified as part of the linearized frame, so the output of positional processing is given in 1.3:

(1.3) $[the]_{DET/definite}$ $[ball]_N$, $[hit]v_{/past}$ $[the]_{DET/definite}$ $[boy]_N$.

The initial evidence for this model, and specifically for its two-stage architecture with the division between functional and positional processing, came from the analysis of speech errors, or slips of the tongue (Garrett, 1975; 1980a; see Bock, 1995). Structural priming provides a lot of the experimental evidence.

Naturalistic speech error data from adult native speakers have been recorded and classified by different investigators, such as Fromkin (1973a; 1973b), Garrett (1975; 1980a; 1980b), and Shattuck-Hufnagel (1979). Garrett (1980a) noted that speech errors obeyed different linguistic constraints and occurred over different stretches of speech, with one set of errors showing sensitivity to semantic and syntactic constraints and spanning longer distances (as in the error in which instead of saying *this seat has a spring in it* the speaker said *this spring has a seat in it*), and another set of errors showing sensitivity to phonological constraints and spanning shorter distances (as in the error: *put it in the par cark* instead of *put it in the car park*). The most interesting observation about speech errors is that they are linguistically constrained. Errors can be classified based on the linguistic element involved and by the type of process (e.g., exchange, blend, addition, omission). We will not review all of the speech error evidence here, for which I refer the reader to Warren (2013). The constraints on errors provide evidence for the staged nature of the production process and the division between grammatical encoding and phonological encoding.

Although there is consensus about the overall architecture of grammatical encoding, there are also areas of disagreement and current debate (for a general introduction to language production, see also Warren, 2013; for a review of grammatical encoding, including past and current debates, see Ferreira et al., 2018; Wheeldon & Konopka, 2023).Three important areas of disagreement that have resulted in modifications of aspects of the model concern: (1) how the activation of information flows through the model, specifically whether it flows strictly in one direction, or whether there is feedback and interactivity; (2) the relationship between lexical and structural processes, whether speakers start sentence formulation as soon as a concept in the message becomes available and activates a lemma (e.g., [boy]), or whether a representation of relational information and the gist of an event, or "what is going on," are a prerequisite for formulation; (3) whether hierarchical relations and linear order are specified in two separate steps, as posited by Garrett (1980a) or whether an alternative *single-stage* view is correct, in which hierarchical relations and linear order are determined at the same time. In Section 2, we will see how structural priming research has contributed to these questions. Because the question of information flow has been strongly been informed by speech error data, we will review it here.

A variant of the consensus production model that includes *cascading* and *interactive* activation (interactive activation model, IAM) was proposed by Dell (1986; see also Dell & Reich, 1981; Dell et al., 1997) for single word access and production. Cascading activation means that downstream levels may also receive activation before all of the upstream levels are done processing (e.g., phonological representations become active even before a lemma is selected). Interactivity means that downstream levels can also send activation back up to higher levels (e.g., active phonological representations may influence lemma selection). The IAM still shares representational assumptions with the two-stage model in that it recognizes distinct levels of representation for lemmas and lexemes, but it differs in the way activation flows. Specifically, prior to having selected a suitable lemma for the message, the phonological level receives activation (via cascading activation) and activation can in turn spread "upstream" and activate lemmas. So, in an IAM, phonological information *can* influence functional/selection processing at the lemma.

The original evidence in support of an IAM came from building different computational models of single word production and getting the models to generate speech errors under different processing assumptions (with/without feedback from phonology). Evidence for or against one particular model comes from comparing the distributions of different kinds of errors obtained from each model to the empirical distributions observed in human speech error corpora. Dell and Reich (1981) computed the frequencies of three different error types: semantic, phonological, and mixed-errors (semantic + phonological, such as saying the word *rat* instead of *cat*). They observed that mixed errors in error corpora occurred too frequently to be accounted for by a model in which phonology and semantics were not allowed to interact. Although the IAM was proposed to account for single word production, an extension of the IAM to sentence production would allow for feedback from the phonology to influence the functional/selectional level in structural processing. In Section 2, we will discuss evidence interactivity from structural priming studies.

2 Structural Priming in Monolingual Adults

2.1 The Use of Structural Priming to Address Representational Questions

Early priming studies were designed to inform models of grammatical encoding. Two important questions addressed via priming are: (1) the division of labor between lexical representations and structural representations; (2) the relationship between semantic representations and syntactic representations. We will review these studies and discuss whether the results are consistent or with the consensus model outlined in Section 1, or whether they suggest modifying the model.

More recently, a general awareness across psycholinguistics of the benefits of having well-powered replications of earlier studies, along with advances in statistical methods, have led researchers to attempt to replicate and extend several of the original priming studies. Recent studies have also extended the use of structural priming paradigms to investigate a broader range of representational questions than they were originally developed for, such as the nature of sentence-level semantic representations. The potential of structural priming as an experimental method to investigate syntax and semantics is increasingly being recognized outside of the psycholinguistics of sentence production.

2.1.1 Priming and the Separation between Lexical and Structural Processing in Sentence Production

The seminal study by Bock (1986b) examined abstract (i.e., lexically independent) priming. Recall that all nouns and verbs differed across prime and target trials: if the prime sentence had the verb *punch* and the nouns were *fans* and *referee* (as in 1.1) target pictures depicted a different kind of action (*strike*) and nominal referents (e.g., *lighting*, *church*).

Additional evidence came from Bock (1989), who also found that primes with the same surface structure primed one another irrespective of whether they shared the same function words (i.e., prepositions): prepositional dative primes (2.1a) containing the preposition (P) *for* were equally good as dative primes (2.1b) containing *to* in eliciting prepositional dative descriptions with *to* (2.1c). This result is consistent with the view that what matters for priming is shared surface syntactic phrase structure (NP-VP-NP-PP) and that there is no additional contribution from function word identity (P = to). We will revisit this finding in Section 2.1.2.

(2.1)   Primes
> a. The secretary baked a cake for her boss (PREPOSITIONAL DATIVE WITH *for*)
> b. The secretary took a cake to his boss (PREPOSITIONAL DATIVE WITH *to*)
>
> Target
> c. The girl is giving a flower to her teacher (PREPOSITIONAL DATIVE WITH *to*)

To more carefully examine the separable contributions of lexical and structural repetition in structural priming, however, one needs to orthogonally manipulate both factors. Priming paradigms are well suited for this. In a series of experiments using structural priming in the written modality, Pickering and Branigan (1998) manipulated sentence structure (DO dative, PO dative) and verb repetition (same verb, different verb) across primes and targets. Participants were given a printed booklet with a list of written sentence fragments, and were asked to complete each fragment in writing with the first thing that came to mind, provided that the fragment and the completion resulted in grammatical sentence in English. In order to make the task as similar as possible on both prime and target trials, primes were also presented as fragments that participants were asked to complete. Prime fragments were constructed so as to bias the structure (DO, PO) with which they could be completed. For example, a prime fragment like 2.2a, where the verb *show* is followed by a direct object makes it more likely that people will complete the sentence with a DO structure. Target fragments ended at the verb (e.g., *showed* ...).

(2.2)   WRITTEN PRIME FRAGMENTS
    a. The racing driver showed the torn overall ... (PO-INDUCING, SAME VERB)
    b. The racing driver showed the helpful mechanic ... (DO-INDUCING, SAME VERB)
    c. The racing driver gave the torn overall ... (PO-INDUCING, SAME VERB)
    d. The racing driver gave the helpful mechanic ... (DO-INDUCING, DIFFERENT VERB)

    TARGET
    e. The patient showed ...

The results showed abstract structural priming – that is, priming when the verbs in the prime were different from the verbs in the targets (e.g., *give* in the prime, *show* in the target). Fragment primes that induced POs (like 2.2c) led to more PO target completions (e.g., *the patient showed the prescription to the doctor*) than did DO-inducing prime fragments. Importantly, Pickering and Branigan (1998) also found an enhanced priming effect when the prime and target used the same verb, (e.g., *show* in the prime and *show* in the target). This enhanced priming effect has since been referred to as the *lexical boost* in structural priming. Before we continue, a terminological observation is in order. Although the original Pickering and Branigan study correctly used the term "verb repetition" to refer to the condition with the same verb in the prime and the target, much subsequent priming literature, including reviews and meta-analyses (e.g., Pickering & Ferreira, 2008; Mahowald et al., 2016) uses the term "overlap" instead of lexical repetition. Following the convention in the later priming literature, we will on occasion use the term *overlap* to refer to conditions where some dimension of the prime (e.g., lexical, semantic, syntactic) is repeated, or shared, between the prime and the target.

In order to test that the locus of priming is indeed at the more abstract grammatical level of the verb *lemma*, not the verb form or *lexeme*, Pickering and Branigan investigated whether repetition of morphological features, specifically tense (2.3a), aspect (2.3b), and number (2.3c) would increase priming magnitude. Recall that in the consensus model the different verb forms in 2.3 (i.e., *show/shows/showed/showing*) are subsumed under one abstract lemma [show]$_v$. None of these additional form manipulations changed the magnitude of the lexically boosted priming effect.

(2.3)   WRITTEN PRIME FRAGMENTS
a. The racing driver shows/the mechanic/the torn overall (DO/PO PRIME, DIFFERENT TENSE)
b. The racing driver was showing/the mechanic/the torn overall (DO/PO PRIME, DIFFERENT ASPECT)
c. The racing drivers show/the mechanic/the torn overall (DO/PO PRIME, DIFFERENT NUMBER)

TARGET
d. The patient showed ...

On the basis of the finding that priming is lexically (verb) independent, priming is boosted when verbs are repeated, but feature repetition does not matter, Pickering and Branigan (1998) argued that the results provide experimental evidence for the lemma/lexeme distinction. They also proposed a modification and extension of the lemma level for the representation of verbs in the consensus model, following up on the lemma model of Roelofs (1992; see Figure 4).

With respect to priming, two important features of Pickering and Branigan's account are that the mechanism assumed for both abstract and lexically boosted priming is activation of lexical-syntactic representations at the lemma level. This account is known as the *residual-activation account* of structural priming. Each verb lemma is linked to its argument structure options in configurations that Pickering and Branigan call combinatorial nodes, as part of a speaker's long-term linguistic memory. So, for example, when a dative verb like *give* is

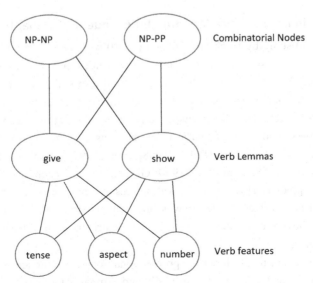

Figure 4 Lexicalist verb lemma model for sentence production.

used in a double object structure (e.g., "Bert gives Ernie a feather"), the NP_NP combinatorial nodes are activated. When *give* is used in the prepositional object ("Bert gives a feather to Ernie"), the NP_PP nodes are activated. Abstract priming is modeled via residual activation of the combinatorial nodes linked to the verb. Lexically boosted priming results from the combined residual activation of the verb lemma and of the combinatorial nodes.

The Pickering and Branigan model integrates a linguistic account of verb argument structure with a psycholinguistic processing model. There is a long tradition in linguistic theory that considers the main verb as the key element in a sentence (Chomsky, 1965; Grimshaw, 1990; Levin, 1993; Levin & Rappaport Hovav, 1995; Pinker, 1989). Because of the central role of the verb in determining its argument structure, this model is lexicalist: it assumes that the meaning and syntax of a sentence are projected from the properties of the main verb.

2.1.2 Priming and the Relationship between Sentence Meaning and Sentence Form

Structural priming paradigms have been employed to investigate what kinds of syntactic and semantic representations and processes are engaged in sentence production. One early line of investigation concerned the separability of syntactic and semantic processing within the framework of the consensus model. Following the priming logic, in these studies, sentence structure is kept constant, and semantic features such as animacy (animate, inanimate entity) or semantic roles such as AGENT, PATIENT or THEME, LOCATION structure vary.

2.1.2.1 Priming Sentence Structure Independent of Semantic Roles

An influential study by Bock and Loebell (1990) was specifically designed to address the relationship between syntax and semantics in sentence production (Experiments 1 and 2). The study also addressed a modularity question with respect to functional and positional processing (Experiment 3). Bock and Loebell (1990) set out to determine whether meaning, expressed in terms of semantic roles, known as *thematic* roles, such as AGENT, PATIENT, THEME, RECIPIENT, or EXPERIENCER (Baker, 1988; 1996; 1997; Bresnan & Kanerva, 1989; Fillmore, 1968; Grimshaw, 1990; Gruber, 1965; Jackendoff, 1972; see Levin & Rappaport Hovav, 2005) was necessary for structural priming, or whether surface syntactic structure was sufficient. To do so, they chose primes and targets that were identical in overall surface structure, but differed in their semantic roles.

In the first experiment, they used prepositional locative sentences (2.4a) and prepositional object dative sentences (2.4b) and compared them to priming after a double object datives (2.4c). In prepositional locative sentences like 2.4a, the semantic role in the prepositional phrase headed by *to* is a DESTINATION, in prepositional datives like 2.4b, the thematic role of the *to*-phrase is a RECIPIENT. Target pictures depicted events with an AGENT, a RECIPIENT, and a THEME. They found that both prepositional locatives and prepositional datives primed prepositional datives, and concluded that structural priming did not require identical semantic roles.

(2.4)   PRIMES
        a. The governor sent a statue of himself to the university (PO-LOCATIVE, DESTINATION)
        b. The governor gave a statue of himself to the university (PO-DATIVE, RECIPIENT)
        c. The governor gave the university a statue of himself (DO-DATIVE)

    TARGET
        d. The boy is throwing a ball to the girl (PO-DATIVE, RECIPIENT)

Although recipients and destinations are considered to be different semantic roles when semantic roles are narrowly defined, some linguistic analyses (e.g., Baker, 1996; Harley, 2003; Goldberg, 1995, 2006; Lakoff & Johnson, 1980; Jackendoff, 1972, 1983; Pylkkänen, 2008) propose a broader definition of semantic roles, based on so-called macro-roles. On a macro-role view, RECIPIENTS and DESTINATIONS are subsumed under a broader role called GOAL. Under a broad thematic role analysis, PO datives and PO locatives would also share a meaning component in addition to shared structure, in that they would have identical thematic roles.

In Experiment 2, Bock and Loebell (1990) provided stronger evidence that thematic role identity is not necessary for priming to occur. In this experiment, they used intransitive locative sentences (2.5a), passive sentences (2.5b), and active controls (2.5c). In intransitive locatives like 2.6a, the thematic role in the *by* phrase is LOCATION, while in passives like 2.5b it is AGENT. Both locative sentences (with *by*) and passives were found to equally prime passive target descriptions. Bock and Loebell took these results as evidence for abstract, purely syntactic priming, as the roles of LOCATION and AGENT are semantically distinct.

(2.5)   PRIMES
        a. The 747 was landing by the control tower (INTRANSITIVE LOCATIVE, *by* LOCATION)
        b. The 747 was alerted by the control tower (PASSIVE, *by* AGENT)
        c. The control tower alerted the 747 (ACTIVE, PATIENT)

    TARGET
        d. The man is awakened by the alarm clock (PASSIVE, *by* AGENT)

One issue related to the design of Bock and Loebell's second experiment is that passive and locative sentences were matched as much as possible, including the preposition (*by*). Is it possible that the homophonous *by* preposition contributed to priming? Bock and Loebell discussed this possibility, but ruled it out based on the study by Bock (1989) that found that varying prepositions within a structural frame did not prevent priming from occurring. We will return to this shortly.

Finally, Bock and Loebell (1990)'s third experiment examined whether priming would occur between sentences that were similar at the positional level but not at the functional level. The stimuli were carefully constructed so that the priming sentences were lexically and phonologically matched down to the identity of the preposition, the number of syllables and lexical stress placement. They used prepositional dative prime sentences like 2.6a and infinitive complement sentences like 2.6b. Beyond the similarities at the positional level, these two sentences have different structural representations. The target pictures were datives events.

(2.6)   PRIMES
        a. Susan brought a book to Stella (PO-DATIVE, *to*)
        b. Susan brought a book to study (INFINITIVE, *to*)

        TARGET
        c. The girl gives a flower to the teacher (PO-DATIVE, *to*)

The results showed priming of prepositional datives (2.6c) after prepositional dative primes, but not after infinitive complement primes. This shows that structural priming does not occur at a "late" positional processing level. With the evidence accrued from this line of experiments, Bock and Loebell (1990) suggested that there is a purely syntactic component to structural priming, reflecting the separation between lexical processing and structure building on the one hand, and semantic processing and syntactic structure building on the other. This evidence is consistent with (and evidence for) the two-stage feed-forward version of the consensus model outlined in Section 1.1.

More recently, Ziegler and colleagues (2019) set out not only to replicate Bock and Loebell (1990)'s second experiment, with a larger sample of participants and updated statistical analyses, but also, crucially, to directly test whether the presence of the overlap in the preposition *by* between the passives and locatives is necessary for priming passives. In addition to using intransitive locative prime sentences containing the preposition *by* (2.7a), they introduced an additional condition in which the intransitive locatives had different types of locative prepositions (e.g., *on*, *near*) that crucially were not *by* (non-*by*, as in 2.7b). Ziegler and colleagues' results confirmed the findings that intransitive locatives with the preposition *by* (2.7a) equally prime *by* passives (2.7e). This replicates and confirms the original Bock and Loebell (1990) finding that structural priming can occur when primes and targets have identical surface syntactic structure, in the absence of semantic (thematic) role identity. However, Ziegler and colleagues also found clear evidence that the identity of the preposition in the PP in the locative prime mattered. Locative primes that had PPs with other prepositions (2.7b) behaved differently from both passive primes and locative primes with *by*, and were no more likely than active control primes (2.7d) to be followed by passive target descriptions.

(2.7)   PRIMES
         a. The 747 was landing by the control tower (INTRANSITIVE LOCATIVE, *by* LOCATION)
         b. The 747 was landing near the control tower (INTRANSITIVE LOCATIVE, non-*by* LOCATION)
         c. The 747 was alerted by the control tower (PASSIVE)
         d. The control tower alerted the 747 (ACTIVE)

       TARGET
         e. The boy is getting hit by a ball (PASSIVE)

These findings are hard to reconcile with previous priming studies, such as Bock's (1989), which argues against a contribution of prepositions in priming. Although not as abstract as originally claimed, the cognitive separability of meaning and form during the process of sentence production is confirmed by these results. Ziegler and colleagues argued that the kinds of linguistic representations required to account for these results must include linguistic representations that contain a combination of abstract lexically independent information along with a lexically specific element (the fact that the head of the prepositional phrase in a full passive must contain the preposition *by*). One such framework is Construction Grammar. Constructions are form-function pairings that exist at different levels of generalization, including representations that are partially lexically filled (Goldberg, 1995; 2006). Constructions are part of a speakers' long-term linguistic knowledge, and importantly, they exist in a network of relations, where different similarity dimensions (form-based or syntactic, and functionally based, or semantic and pragmatic) serve to link constructions that overlap on one or more dimensions.

2.1.2.2 Separable Priming Effects of Sentence Structure and Animacy-to-Subject Mappings

Separable, additive effects of structure and animacy were found by Bock, Loebell, and Morey (1992), in an elegant design with materials that combined a structure manipulation (active and passive) and an animacy manipulation in the primes leading to a set of priming conditions shown in 2.8. Animacy features of surface grammatical subjects varied systematically: they were animate in two priming sentences, one active (2.8a) and one passive (2.8d), and inanimate in the other two, again, one active (2.8c) and one passive (2.8b). Targets were always images depicting transitive events with an inanimate AGENT and an animate PATIENT (e.g., an alarm clock awakening a boy, a bicycle hitting a pedestrian).

(2.8)   PRIMES
    a. Five people carried the boat (ACTIVE, ANIMATE SUBJECT)
    b. The boat was carried by five people (PASSIVE, INANIMATE SUBJECT)
    c. The boat carried five people (ACTIVE, INANIMATE SUBJECT)
    d. Five people were carried by the boat (PASSIVE, ANIMATE SUBJECT)

    TARGET
    e. The bicycle hits the pedestrian (ACTIVE, INANIMATE SUBJECT)

Speakers were found to be more likely to describe target pictures with the structure of the prime, irrespective of animacy. Specifically, on average, they produced more active sentences (like 2.8e) after active primes (2.8a and 2.8c) than after passive primes (2.8b and 2.8e). But speakers also persisted in mapping similar animacy features onto grammatical subjects, irrespective of sentence structure. Primes that had inanimate subjects, irrespective of whether the sentences were active or passive (2.8b and 2.8c), were more likely to elicit targets with inanimate subjects than were primes with animate subjects (2.8a and 2.8d). The study also had an instruction manipulation where participants were assigned either to a focus on form condition or focus on meaning condition. The form and meaning focus instruction concerned the running recognition memory task. Participants were told that they would hear sentences with nearly identical meanings to those of previously heard sentences, but with different wordings. In the form-focused instruction, they were told to pay closer attention to how sentences were worded, so sentences that had similar meanings but different wordings should be recognized as different. In the meaning-focused instruction, they were given the opposite instructions (i.e., that if sentences had similar meanings but different wordings, they should be recognized as being the same). While the instruction manipulation had an effect on the magnitude of the effects (stronger structural persistence was found under form-focused instructions, as to be expected), it did not change the overall pattern of the results.

Chen and colleagues (2022), following the original Bock and colleagues (1992) design as closely as possible, replicated both findings, structural and animacy, with no interaction between the two. The finding that the effects of structure and animacy were additive and not interactive, supports the view that structural priming and conceptual (animacy) priming are independent of each other. Bock and colleagues considered syntax to be the locus of structural persistence, but the fact that actives primed actives and passives prime passives does not unequivocally demonstrate this, as actives and passives also differ from each other in terms of semantic role order (agent patient/theme order in activesvs. patient/theme agent in passives), and pragmatics (focus on the patient/theme in passives).

2.1.2.3 Priming Semantic Role Order Independent of Syntactic Constituent Order

Priming studies have also shown priming of semantic structure above and beyond priming of surface syntactic structure (e.g., Bernolet, Hartsuiker, & Pickering, 2009; Chang, Bock, & Goldberg, 2003; Griffin & Weinstein-Tull, 2003; Ziegler, Snedeker, & Wittenberg, 2018).

Chang, Bock, and Goldberg (2003) examined whether the order in which different semantic roles occur in a sentence can be primed for sentences that have the same surface syntax. They used sentence primes that both had NP-V-NP-PP order, but with different semantic role orders: THEME–LOCATION in one condition (2.9a), and LOCATION–THEME in the other (2.9b).

(2.9) PRIMES
  a. The maid rubbed polish onto the table (NP-PP THEME–LOCATION order)
  b. The maid rubbed the table with polish (NP-PP LOCATION–THEME order)

  TARGET
  c. The farmer heaped straw onto the wagon (NP-PP THEME–LOCATION order)

They found that THEME–LOCATION primes (2.9a) primed THEME–LOCATION targets (2.9c), more than LOCATION–THEME (2.9b) primes did, despite their identical syntax. These results show that structural priming can be sensitive to semantic relations, in addition to syntax.

Griffin and Weinstein-Tull (2003) also found evidence of semantic priming, again, while controlling for surface syntax. They exploited a semantic difference between two superficially similar types of complement clauses in English, called *object raising* (2.10a) and *object control* structures (2.10b), after the type of predicate in the main clause. Both raising and control predicates in 2.10 select for a verb phrase complement in the infinitive form (*to fix the car*), and the sentences have identical surface syntax (NP$_{subject}$ V NP$_{object}$ infinitive VP). The structures, however, differ with respect to the properties of the object NP. Crucially for the purposes of this study, raising predicates do not assign a semantic role to their objects, but control predicates do. In 2.10a, "Pat" has no semantic role in the main clause ("Pat" isn't "being expected," it is the whole event "Pat fixing the car" that is expected). "Pat" only has an AGENT role in the complement clause, as the agent of "to fix the car." In 2.10b, "Pat" has both an AGENT role in the complement clause and an EXPERIENCER role in main clause

("Pat" is both "the one being persuaded" and the agent of "fix the car"). In some linguistic analysis, the difference between raising and control structures is captured syntactically, by assuming that they involve two different types of syntactic operations: movement for raising structures, and control for control structures. In the raising case in 2.10a, "Pat" is assumed to originate as the subject of the complement clause, and then move to the object position of the main clause verb for syntactic reasons. In the control case in 2.10b, no movement is involved. "Pat" originates in object position in the main clause and controls the subject position of the embedded clause.

(2.10) a. Kim expected Pat to fix the car (OBJECT RAISING, INFINITIVE COMPLEMENT)
        b. Kim persuaded Pat to fix car (OBJECT CONTROL, INFINITIVE COMPLEMENT)

Griffin and Weinstein-Tull (2003) primed object raising sentences with infinitive clauses, using a sentence recall version of the priming task (Potter and Lombardi, 1998). Participants were asked to recall object raising sentences that contained finite complements (2.10a) after being primed with object raising sentences (2.11a) and object control sentences (2.11b), both containing infinitive complements. On a semantic priming account, it should be possible to detect the effect of the additional semantic "match" between object raising primes and object target structures, when compared to object control primes because the latter have an additional semantic role.

(2.11) SENTENCE TO BE RECALLED
        a. The police suspected that Joan was the criminal (OBJECT RAISING, FINITE COMPLEMENT)

        PRIMES
        b. A teaching assistant reported the exam to be too difficult (OBJECT RAISING, INFINITIVE COMPLEMENT)
        c. Rover begged his owner to be more generous with food (OBJECT CONTROL, INFINITIVE COMPLEMENT)

        TARGET
        d. The police suspected Joan to be the criminal (OBJECT RAISING, INFINITIVE COMPLEMENT)

The results confirmed the predictions: when recalling object raising finite sentences, participants produced more object raising infinitives after object raising infinitive primes, than after object control infinitive primes. The authors suggested they detected a semantic priming effect beyond surface syntactic priming, specifically due to the extra semantic role in object control infinitive primes, which makes these structures semantically different from object raising sentences.

2.1.2.4 Priming Information Structure

Languages provide speakers with the option of expressing the same basic ideas in different ways. The sentences in 2.12 convey the same relational meaning ("someone named Pat lost their keys") but the way this meaning is presented varies in its *information structure* (Lambrecht, 1994; for an overview, see Griffiths, 2006). Information structure constructions allow speakers to foreground or focus certain elements in the sentence more than others, with morphosyntactic and or prosodic means. Depending on the communicative context, some ways of presenting information will be more pragmatically appropriate than others, and this depends crucially on what the speaker assumes the hearer already knows, or can infer, about a given situation (background, old, presupposed, or topical information) and what the speaker assumes the hearer does not know (new, asserted, or focused).

(2.12)   a. Pat lost her keys in the garden last night
        b. It was Pat who lost her keys in the garden last night (*IT*-CLEFT, AGENT-FOCUS)
        c. It was her keys that Pat lost in the garden last night (*IT*-CLEFT, PATIENT-FOCUS)

Structural priming has seldom been used to examine information structure. As mentioned in Section 1.1, structural priming studies rely on presenting pictures in isolation and eliciting single sentences, outside of a discourse context, so they may not be ideal to examine information structure. There are, in fact, more suitable methods for examining what speakers produce when different portions of an event are focused, such as asking questions "what is happening to the X," what is X doing to Y," or eliciting longer stretches of discourse or conversation, while varying the discourse status of referents or events.

One study that did employ priming to examine information structure was conducted in Dutch (Vernice, Pickering, & Hartsuiker, 2012). The study found that sentences with an information structure that focuses the PATIENT (the authors use the term "emphasis"), such as *it*-clefts and *wh*-clefts (2.13a–2.13c), were more likely to prime passive sentence descriptions than *it*-clefts and *wh*-clefts that focused on the AGENT (2.13d–2.13cf). The important finding is that patient-focused sentences primed passive picture descriptions, despite the fact that passives, *it*-clefts, and *wh*-clefts have different syntactic forms. These results add to the evidence that structural priming is not exclusively a syntactic phenomenon.

(2.13)   PRIMES
        a. Het is de cowboy die hij slaat (*IT*-CLEFT, PATIENT-FOCUS)
           [It is the cowboy that he is hitting]
        b. Degene die hij slaat is de cowboy (*WH*-CLEFT, PATIENT-FOCUS)

[The one who he is hitting is the cowboy]

  c. De cowboy is degene die hij slaat (INVERTED *WH*-CLEFT, PATIENT-FOCUS)
     [The cowboy is the one who he is hitting]

  d. Het is de cowboy die hem slaat (*IT*-CLEFT, AGENT-FOCUS)
     [It is the cowboy that is hitting him]

  e. Degene die hem slaat is de cowboy (*WH*-CLEFT, AGENT-FOCUS)
     [The one who is hitting him is the cowboy]

  f. De cowboy is degene die hem slaat (INVERTED *WH*-CLEFT, AGENT-FOCUS)
     [The cowboy is the one who is hitting him]

TARGET

  g. De jongen wordt geraakt door de bal (PASSIVE, PATIENT-FOCUS)
     [The boy is getting hit by the ball]

2.1.3 Interim Summary

We have reviewed some of the classic priming literature developed to address representational questions with respect to the architecture of sentence production, along with more recent replications and extensions. The two "classic" questions concern the possibility of using priming to probe the separation of content and structure processing in production, both at the lexical level (lexical vs. abstract priming) and with respect to syntax and semantics. Lexically independent (abstract) priming provides evidence that structure is represented as a separate level from lexical content. The fact that priming taps into the lemma level and not the lexeme (Section 2.1.1), also provides converging evidence for this distinction in the consensus model. Bock and Loebell (1990), and the replication by Ziegler and colleagues (2019), demonstrate the separability of syntactic processing from semantic processing in production. We have seen that priming of syntactic structure can be independent of priming of semantic structure, and vice-versa, priming of semantic structure can occur independently from syntactic structure.

Although these findings are consistent with the overall architecture of the consensus sentence production model outlined in Section 2.1, Ziegler and colleagues' results are a challenge for the feed-forward version: one has to be able to account for the fact that sentences whose linearized structural frames contained the preposition *by* primed *by*-passives, but sentences with identical linearized structural frames but different prepositions did not prime *by*-passives. One way to account for this result is to assume interactivity in the production model. Upon hearing a prime with the locative preposition *by*, activation from the phonological level and feedback from this level to the grammatical encoding level makes it more likely that the speaker will produce a passive sentence with a *by* phrase. This is not the same thing as stating that the effect is purely lexical (i.e., that *by* alone would necessarily prime a passive). This account still assumes that when *by* is embedded in the right structural representation, it can act as a cue for a passive sentence structure. It is also important to keep in mind that in the context of a production priming experiment, target pictures themselves (sketches of events with an AGENT and a PATIENT or THEME) are already compatible with the generation of a message with the semantics and pragmatics of a passive.

2.1.4 Priming to Examine Whether Grammatical Encoding Is Two-Staged

The consensus model outlined in Section 1 is a two-stage model. It assumes a level of representation where grammatical relations (e.g., subject, object) are specified without linear order. As mentioned in Section 1, there is debate as to whether this two-step architecture is necessary. The relatively inflexible word order of English, however, makes it hard to disentangle whether conceptual features and semantic roles map onto grammatical positions such as subject and object, whether they map onto linearized order, or both. For example, in Bock and colleagues' (1992) study, the additive effect of animacy and structural transitive (active/passive) priming could be an effect of priming the mapping of animacy to subject, but also of priming animacy to linear position, specifically first mention in the sentence. Chang and colleagues' study (2003), showing priming of semantic roles is compatible with a mapping from semantic role to grammatical position, but also with a mapping from semantic role to linear position.

Pickering and colleagues (2002) tried to disentangle mapping of concept to grammatical position from mapping of concept to linear position in English using PO-datives, DO-datives, and so-called shifted-PO datives. Shifted-PO datives have the same hierarchical structure as non-shifted PO datives, but differ in their linear orders (see 2.14c compared with 2.14b).

(2.14) a. The racing driver showed the helpful mechanic the damaged wheel (DO)
        b. The racing driver showed the damaged wheel to the helpful mechanic (PO)
        c. The racing driver showed to the helpful mechanic the damaged wheel (SHIFTED-PO)
        d. The racing driver fainted ... (INTRANSITIVE CONTROL)

They found that shifted-PO datives were no more likely to prime PO datives than intransitive control prime sentences (2.14d). Pickering and colleagues (2002) took these results to be consistent with a one-stage view of sentence production.

Cai, Pickering, and Branigan (2012) exploited the more flexible word-order options in Mandarin Chinese to again disentangle mapping of concept to grammatical position from mapping of concept to linear position. They employed "regular" DO and PO datives (2.15a, 2.15b), topicalized DO and PO datives (2.15c, 2.15d), and a construction called *Ba*-DO (2.15e) in which the direct object of a DO appears before the verb, with the meaning of affectedness. This option is only available for DO structures, not POs. Topicalized POs and regular POs are similar with respect to how they map semantic roles to grammatical functions, but differ with respect to linearized positions. In both regular POs and topicalized POs, themes are mapped onto direct objects and recipients onto indirect objects, but in topicalized POs the direct object appears sentence initially. Topicalized POs and topicalized DOs, instead, differ in their functional role mappings, with topicalized POs behaving like regular POs, and topicalized DOs like regular DOs. However, they share linear semantic role order (THEME-AGENT-RECIPIENT). *Ba*-DO sentences share thematic to linear order mappings with regular POs (AGENT-RECIPIENT-THEME), but not thematic to grammatical function mappings, which they instead share with regular DOs.

(2.15)   a. Niuzai song-gei le shuishou naben (DO)
            cowboy give-to LE sailor the book
            [The cowboy gave the sailor the book]
    b. Niuzai song-gei le shuishou naben (PO)
            cowboy give-to LE sailor the book
            [The cowboy gave the sailor the book]
    c. Naben shu niuzai song-gei le shuishou (TOPICALIZED-DO)
            the book cowboy give-to LE sailor
            [The book the cowboy gave the sailor]
    d. Naben shu niuzai song le gei shuishou (TOPICALIZED-PO)
            the book cowboy give LE to sailor
            [The book the cowboy gave (it) to the sailor]
    e. Niuzai ba naben shu song-gei le shuishou (*Ba*-DO)
            cowboy BA the book give-to LE sailor
            [The cowboy gave the sailor the book]

Cai and colleagues (2012) found evidence of both thematic role to grammatical role priming and thematic role to linear order priming. Topicalized POs (2.15c) primed POs (2.15b), showing thematic role to grammatical function priming, despite differences in word order. Topicalized DOs (2.15c) also primed POs, showing thematic role to linear order priming, despite different grammatical functions. They also found that *Ba*-DO primes (2.15e) primed PO rather than DO sentences. Ba-DO sentences and and POs share mappings of thematic role to linear position but not of thematic role to grammatical function.

    Taken together, these results show evidence that evidence of priming from concept (semantic role) both to grammatical function and to linear position, showing that speakers are sensitive to both kinds of mappings during language production. These results support a view of grammatical encoding with separable levels: one for function assignment and hierarchical structure and another one for linearized order.

2.1.5 Priming to Investigate Semantic Representations

Although earlier priming studies sought to investigate the nature of the syntactic representations required to account for language production, more recently priming has been employed to investigate the nature of linguistic semantic representations. From a psycholinguistic point of view, such studies provide information about the conceptual-semantic dimensions that influence the mapping between messages and grammatical encoding.

2.1.5.1 Priming to determine whether Semantic Roles are Broad or Narrow

Recall the priming results of Bock and Loebell (1990; see Section 2.1.2.2) that prepositional locatives (with a destination role) primed prepositional datives (with a recipient role), which can be accounted for either by assuming that structural priming does not depend on identical semantic roles (as the authors did), or alternatively, that semantics are also at play, but under a broader view of semantic roles where a broad GOAL role subsumes RECIPIENTS and DESTINATIONS.

Ziegler and Snedeker (2018) used structural priming to further explore this question, asking whether speakers rely on broad thematic roles, or whether roles are more specific. Across a series of experiments, they examined priming between datives and locatives (THEME–LOCATION/LOCATION–THEME orders, as in Chang et al., 2003). In addition, they manipulated the animacy of the LOCATION role (animate/inanimate). If speakers represent semantic relations only relying on broad thematic roles, speakers should be insensitive to the more fine-grained distinction between RECIPIENTS (2.16a, 2.16b) and LOCATIONS (2.16c, 2.16d), because these roles are subsumed under the broad role called GOAL. On a broad semantic-role hypothesis, then, datives should prime locatives and vice-versa, irrespective of animacy.

(2.16) PRIME AND TARGET SENTENCE TYPES
   a. The boy hands the suitcase to his mother (PO: THEME + GOAL [RECIPIENT])
   b. The boy hands his mother the suitcase (DO: GOAL[RECIPIENT] + THEME)
   c. The boy loads the bag on the cart (THEME–LOCATION order: THEME + inanimate GOAL [DESTINATION])
   d. The boy loads the cart with the bag (LOCATION–THEME order: inanimate GOAL [DESTINATION] + THEME)

e. The boy sprayed cologne on the man (THEME–LOCATION order: THEME + animate GOAL [DESTINATION])

f. The boy sprayed the man with cologne (LOCATION–THEME order: animate GOAL [DESTINATION] + THEME)

The results showed that datives primed datives and locatives primed locatives. For locative-to-dative and dative-to-locative priming, the presence of a priming effect depended crucially on the animacy feature of the GOAL. Locatives had to have an animate GOAL (2.16e, 2.16f), therefore matching the animacy features in datives, for priming to occur, otherwise no priming was found. These results are at odds with the broad view thematic roles. They provide evidence that recipients and DESTINATIONS have distinct semantic representations, as proposed by many theorists (Bresnan & Kanerva, 1989; Pinker, 1989; Rappaport Hovav & Levin, 2008; Levin & Rappaport Hovav, 2005). This supports the original interpretation of the Bock and Loebell (1990) experiment that prepositional locative and prepositional dative priming was due to overlapping structure, not semantics.

The finding that animacy exerts an independent effect on priming is in line with previous findings (Bock et al., 1992; Chen et al., 2022) and adds to the literature reviewed above that different similarity dimensions above and beyond structural similarity can be involved in structural priming in production.

2.1.5.2 Priming Different Verb Senses at the Lemma Level

Bernolet, Colleman, and Hartsuiker (2014) examined whether a verb's semantic sense is also subject to priming. They tested dative (DO/PO) priming in Dutch, with dative verbs with different senses, for example 2.17a, where the verb appears in its literal prototypical sense involving physical transfer of a theme to a recipient, and 2.17b, where the sense of the verb is abstract and the meaning is non- compositional and idiomatic (i.e., "to give someone a heart attack" means "to frighten" or "to shock"). Targets were always prototypical physical transfer scenes. They found a sense boost to structural priming: priming was larger when prime and target also shared the same verb sense.

(2.17) PRIMES

a. De kok bezorgt de matroos een hoed/een hoed aan de matroos
[The cook gives the sailor a hat/a hat to the sailor] (DO/PO LITERAL DATIVES, SAME SENSE)

b. De bokser bezorgt de rechter een hartaanval/een hartaanval aan de rechter
[The boxer gives the judge a heart attack/a heart attack to the judge] (DO/PO IDIOMATIC DATIVES, DIFFERENT SENSE)

TARGET PICTURE
painter, cowboy, ball, give (LITERAL DATIVE)

Bernolet and colleagues (2014) also looked at whether verb form repetition itself (independent of sense repetition) contributes to the lexical boost effect. Verb identity (same/different verb) was manipulated while holding sense constant: targets were pictures of the prototypical concrete transfer senses, while verbs in the primes had either a metaphorical or a transfer sense. A significant boost to priming was found in all conditions with verb form (lexeme) repetition. Taken together, these results show that there are separate contributions to the lexical (verb) boost effect: one that comes from the meaning component (verb sense) and one that comes from the verb lexeme.

One way in which the Pickering and Branigan (1998) verb lemma model can account for these results is to assume the Lemma Argument Probability Hypothesis (Roland & Jurafsky, 2002). Based on analysis of naturalistic and experimental corpora, Roland & Jurafsky (2002) determined that verb bias – that is, the probability with which verbs occur in different argument structures – (e.g., whether a dative verb occurs in the DO or PO) depends on verb sense. They proposed an extension of the lemma model with two additional features: one is to have separate but semantically related lemmas for different verb senses connected to the same lexemes. In addition, to account for sense-specific differences in verb bias, the links between sense lemmas and combinatorial nodes are differentially weighted.

2.1.5.3 Priming Semantic Event Structures

In describing the consensus model for sentence production in Section 1.1 and in the priming studies examined thus far, we have relied on semantic representations for verbs and sentences that follow a long tradition in the field of linguistics of assuming as primitive constructs classic thematic roles such as AGENT, PATIENT, and RECIPIENT (e.g., Baker, 1988, 1996, 1997; Bresnan & Kanerva, 1989; Fillmore, 1968; Dowty, 1991; Grimshaw, 1990; Gruber, 1965 Jackendoff, 1972).

There are, however, alternative theories of verb and sentence semantics based on verb event structures (Goldberg, 1995; Jackendoff, 1990, 2002; Pinker, 1989; Rappport Hovav & Levin, 1998; 2011; c.f. Levin & Rappoport Hovav, 2005). In event semantic theories of verb representation, each verb argument structure has an associated *event structure* expressed via primitive predicates that can be embedded within each other, such as ACT, BE, HAVE, BECOME, CAUSE, and MOVE. So, for example, the proposed event structure representation of a transitive verb like *kick* is [X ACT on Y]. For a dative verb like *give* in its DO argument structure, the proposed event representation has CAUSE predicate with an embedded HAVE predicate: X CAUSE [Y HAVE Z]. In its PO argument structure, a different event structure is proposed that consists of a CAUSE predicate with an embedded BE as predicate: X CAUSE [Y BE at Z]. Is it possible to use structural priming to adjudicate between these different hypotheses about the nature of semantic representations in sentence production?

Ziegler, Snedeker, and Wittenberg (2018) aimed to do this. They used three different types of datives: compositional, light verb, and idiomatic datives exemplified in 2.18.

(2.18)   a. Miss Piggy gives Kermit a feather/a feather to Kermit (COMPOSITIONAL)
           b. Miss Piggy gives Kermit a hug/a hug to Kermit (LIGHT VERB)
           c. Miss Piggy gives Kermit the cold shoulder/the cold shoulder to Kermit (IDIOMATIC)

All sentences employed the verb *give* so that materials could be balanced across conditions. It is important to keep in mind that all three types of datives have the same surface syntactic structure. Where they differ is in their meaning. When *give* is used as a main verb in PO and DO compositional datives (2.18a), from a semantic point of view, three participants are involved. The meaning of compositional dative typically entails transfer of the theme from the AGENT to the RECIPIENT (e.g., the DO version of 2.18a can be paraphrased as "Miss Piggy causes a feather to be transferred to Kermit"). When *give* is used as a light verb or in an idiomatic dative construction, the meaning is quite different from compositional datives. Semantically, both light verb and idiomatic datives are two-participant events, with an AGENT and a PATIENT role (2.18b can be paraphrased as "Miss Piggy hugs Kermit" and 2.18c as "Miss Piggy is ignoring Kermit").

To adjudicate between the two semantic accounts, Ziegler and colleagues (2018) set up their predictions based on the differences in the semantic representations proposed for compositional, idiomatic, and light verb datives according to the two theories of verb and sentence semantics. We will spell each representation out, starting from a semantic role account.

On a classic semantic role account, DO datives are characterized by a mapping from the recipient role to the first direct object 1 (NP1) and the theme to the second object (NP2) (2.19a). PO datives have a theme-to-direct object and recipient-to-oblique mapping (2.19b). For light verb and for idiomatic datives (recall that these meanings are two-place predicate relations), the semantic role account posits that the patient role is mapped onto the direct-object (NP1) for DOs (2.19c, 2.19e) and onto the oblique for POs (2.19d).

(2.19)   *Semantic role account of compositional, light verb, and idiomatic datives*
   a. Miss Piggy gives Kermit a feather (COMPOSITIONAL DO: RECIPIENT-NP I; THEME-NP2)
   b. Miss Piggy gives a feather to Kermit (COMPOSITIONAL PO: THEME-NP I; RECIPIENT-OBLIQUE)
   c. Miss Piggy gives Kermit a hug (LIGHT VERB DO: PATIENT-NP I)
   d. Miss Piggy gives a hug to Kermit (LIGHT VERB PO: PATIENT-OBLIQUE)
   e. Miss Piggy gives Kermit the cold shoulder (IDIOMATIC VERB DO: PATIENT-NP I)
   f. Miss Piggy gives the cold shoulder to Kermit (IDIOMATIC VERB PO: PATIENT-OBLIQUE)

Let's turn now to the event structure representations (2.20). The event structures posited by linguists for compositional datives are: x CAUSE [y HAVE z] for DOs, and: X CAUSE [Y BE at Z] for POs. For idiomatic datives, the same event semantic representation is assumed for both DOs and POs [X ACT on Z].

(2.20)   *Event structure account of compositional, light verb, and idiomatic datives*
   a. Miss Piggy gives Kermit a feather (COMPOSITIONAL DO: X CAUSE [Y HAVE Z])
   b. Miss Piggy gives a feather to Kermit (COMPOSITIONAL PO: X CAUSE [Y BE at Z])
   c. Miss Piggy gives Kermit a hug (LIGHT VERB DO: [X ACT on Z])
   d. Miss Piggy gives a hug to Kermit (LIGHT VERB PO: [X ACT on Z])
   e. Miss Piggy gives Kermit the cold shoulder (IDIOMATIC VERB DO: [X ACT on Z])
   f. Miss Piggy gives the cold shoulder to Kermit (IDIOMATIC VERB PO: [X ACT on Z])

In a first experiment, Ziegler and colleagues primed compositional dative targets with compositional, idiomatic, and light verb primes. The examples from 2.18 are shown again here for ease of presentation.

(2.21)   PRIMES
   a.   Miss Piggy gives Kermit a feather/a feather to Kermit (COMPOSITIONAL)
   b.   Miss Piggy gives Kermit a hug/a hug to Kermit (LIGHT VERB)
   c.   Miss Piggy gives Kermit the cold shoulder/the cold shoulder to Kermit (IDIOMATIC)

   TARGET
   d.   Big Bird gives Julia a turtle/a turtle to Julia (COMPOSITIONAL)

The results showed priming effects from light verb (2.21b) and idiomatic (2.21c) datives to compositional datives (2.21d), with compositional DOs more likely after light verb or idiomatic DOs than after light verb or idiomatic POs. This effect can be accounted for based on shared surface syntactic structure. Crucially, there was also enhanced priming from compositional dative primes (2.21a), an effect that the authors attributed to an effect of semantics, above and beyond surface syntax. This enhanced priming effect, due to the identical semantic structure of the prime and the target (both compositional), is equally predicted by the semantic role account and the event structure account, so priming between compositional datives cannot adjudicate between the two theories. But it does add to the evidence that semantic structure can be primed in addition to surface syntax.

In a second experiment, Ziegler and colleagues examined priming from compositional and light verb dative primes to compositional and light verb targets. The light verb DO and the light verb PO have different semantic representations according to the semantic role account (patient-to-direct-object, patient-to-oblique, respectively), but have identical representations according to the semantic role account (X ACT on Z). Assuming that semantics matters above and beyond surface-syntax (as established in Experiment 1) the prediction was that only datives that have this additional meaning similarity will exhibit enhanced priming compared to when they do not. The results aligned with these predictions. Ziegler and colleagues (2018) took these priming results to support an event structure account of verb semantics.

2.2 Why Does Structural Priming Occur?

Thus far, we have looked structural priming studies that were aimed at representational questions. These studies have contributed greatly to our understanding of the architecture of the sentence production system, specific-ally the stage called grammatical encoding. We also saw that structural priming is useful for the experimental investigation of linguistic representa-tions in adults. In Sections 3 and 4, we will also see how priming applies to investigating representational questions in children and speakers of more than one language.

In this sub-section, we will follow another important line of inquiry into the functions and the cognitive mechanisms of structural priming in adult speakers. Two different perspectives on priming have contributed to this topic: one comes from the study of priming in dialogue settings, the other one comes from connecting priming to life-long language learning. We will examine each perspective in turn.

2.2.1 Priming as a Mechanism for Alignment in Dialogue

Pickering and Garrod (2004, see also Pickering & Garrod, 2013) were the first to propose that the functions of priming, both lexical and structural, are best understood within the context of a psycholinguistic theory of dialogue.

The psycholinguistic model of dialogue is called the *interactive alignment model*. Pickering and Garrod propose that during communicative activities speakers align representations at multiple levels: phonetic-phonological, lexical, semantic-pragmatic, and syntactic. On this view, structural priming is an abstract and implicit form of alignment. Because the mechanism is implicit and automatic, it does not require deliberate allocation of resources, thus serving the function of making an incredibly complex task (comprehending and producing language) easier for both producers and comprehenders.

Pickering and Garrod's alignment model is massively interactive: they assume interactivity between all levels of representation, both within interlocutors and between them. Alignment at one level (e.g., lexical) leads to alignment at other levels (e.g., syntactic), which is the explanation for the lexical boost effect. Pickering and Garrod argue that production in monologue settings (the classic approach to the study of sentence production) is only a special case of dialogue. What distinguishes monologue from dialogue is the amount of alignment between interlocutors. Alignment (via priming) is the reason why speakers can often complete their interlocutor's sentences and why the units of analysis in dialogue may not be the classic model of a sentence produced from scratch. The prediction of this account, is therefore, that priming effects in dialogue settings should be greater than in monologue settings. This prediction is borne out.

Branigan, Pickering, and Cleland (2000) developed a priming paradigm suitable for the experimental study of priming in dialogue. This paradigm has been hugely successful in eliciting priming effects in adults. The "priming in dialogue paradigm", called *confederate scripting*, involves the presence of an interlocutor who, unbeknownst to the participants, is a confederate of the experimenter and provides the primes. In this classic dialogue paradigm, the confederate and the participant sit at table across from each other, and play a dialogue game involving cards to be described, placed in front of them. A screen between them prevents them from seeing each other's cards (see Figure 5).

Instructions to the participants specify that the goal of the study is to understand how people communicate when they cannot see each other. To make the game setup of the experiment work, at the beginning of the experiment, participant and confederate are presented with two ordered sets of cards each: a set of cards to be described placed face down in a box. This is the description set. The other set of cards is already displayed in an array, face up in front of the participant. This is the selection set. When the confederate describes a picture, the participant has to verify whether the description matches any of the pictures in their selection set. If it does, the card is then placed into a discard box.

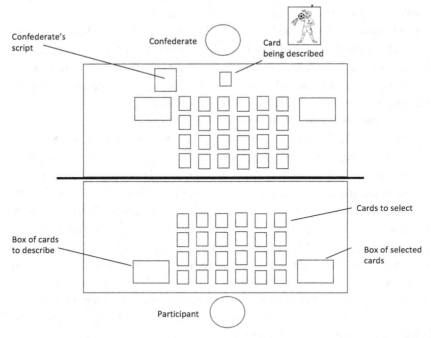

Figure 5 Typical setup for a spoken sentence dialogue production priming study with a live confederate.

The confederate follows a predetermined script in describing the cards, and the form of the confederate's description (e.g., active/passive, DO/PO) is systematically manipulated. This is the equivalent of a priming manipulation in monologue. Using the confederate-scripting technique, it has been possible to show that structural priming effects are much larger in dialogue settings than in monologue settings. Confederate scripting techniques can be adapted to examine how sentence production is influenced by many interactional, social, and sociolinguistic variables, which are harder to study in monologue settings.

Hartsuiker and colleagues (2008) developed a computerized written dialogue variant of the of the priming paradigm with a confederate. Instead of sitting in front of a real person like in the face-to-face dialogue version, participants were told they are chatting live via the computer with a real person in another room. The task was to describe pictures to each other using the chat line, and to verify each others' descriptions. The scripted set of primes was predetermined and typed out by the computer, instead of a real interlocutor. Hartsuiker and colleagues (2008) primed datives (PO/DO) with and without verb overlap, and found large priming and lexical repetition (verb repetition) effects in the written dialogue paradigm. Importantly, these effects were comparable in magnitude to the priming and lexical repetition effects observed in spoken dialogue and much larger than those found in written monologue (Pickering and Branigan, 1998) and spoken monologue (Branigan et al., 2000) versions. In two additional experiments, Hartsuiker and colleagues also examined the time-course of priming effects, which leads to the next important set of questions developed in the priming literature, concerning priming mechanisms.

2.2.2 Abstract Structural Priming as Implicit Learning

In all of the priming studies reviewed this far, prime sentences immediately preceded targets (i.e., there was no additional intervening material between prime and target). One important question addressed in this section concerns the duration of priming effects, as it turns out that answers to this question provide information about the mechanisms that support priming.

Studies that examine the duration of structural priming often use the term "long-term" or long-lasting" to refer to priming effects that persist when the prime and the target are separated either by intervening distractor trials, or a short time interval, in the order of minutes. This differs from other areas of psychology, where long-term priming is defined on the scale of days or weeks (Moutsopoulou et al., 2019). We will follow the convention adopted in the structural priming literature and talk about long-term priming even when it occurs on this shorter time-scale for simplicity and consistency with the primary literature. Although there are important reasons to examine the effects of priming over longer time-scales, especially in studies that use priming proced-ures as an intervention, the question of whether priming decays immediately, or whether it persists over distractor trials, has provided crucial information to understand how priming works and how it is connected to learning.

Starting from the 2000s, a number of studies examined whether priming decays rapidly or whether it persists over intervening filler trials. Bock and Griffin (2000) examined the time-course of abstract priming with active/passive, and DO/PO primes and targets in a paradigm in which a variable number of filler trials (up to 10) was inserted between the prime and the target (See Figure 6). Fillers were constructed so as not to compete directly with either active/passive or DO/PO priming, so they included a variety of sentence structures but did not include transitive or dative sentences. Likewise, pictures were chosen so as to not lead to transitive or dative descriptions. Priming effects were found at all lags (from lag 0 to lag 10), and interestingly, the magnitude of these effects was undiminished over lags.

Recall that the Residual Activation Model of structural priming (Pickering & Branigan,1998; see also Cleland & Pickering, 2003) was proposed to account

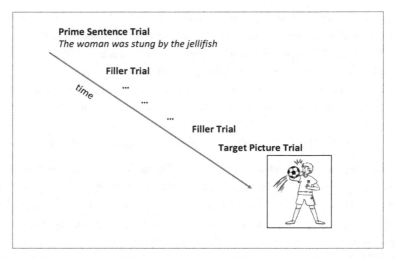

Figure 6 Typical sequence of events in a structural priming experiment with a lag manipulation.

for both abstract and lexically boosted priming. Abstract priming was due to residual activation of the combinatorial nodes connected to the verb lemma, the lexical boost effect came from the combined residual activation of a repeated verb lemma node and the residual activation of the link between the lemma node and the combinatorial nodes. Because activation decays rapidly, a purely activation-based account predicts that priming should decay rapidly with time or interfering trials. Bock and Griffin took their results to argue against an account of priming that relies only on Residual Activation, and suggested an account that views priming as the reflection of the implicit ability of the production system to adapt or change in response to linguistic experience. In other words, they proposed that priming was a form of implicit learning. Additional studies have compared the magnitude and time course of priming effects in versions of the task where participants repeat the prime (see Bock & Griffin, 2000) to those observed in variants of the task where participants don't repeat the prime (Bock et al., 2007) finding similar effects (for relative clauses, see Tooley & Bock, 2014; for actives and passives, see Litcofsky & van Hell, 2019). In an important study comparing the time-course of abstract priming and lexically boosted priming over lags (0, 2, 4, and 6) in both the spoken and the written modality, Hartsuiker and colleagues (2008) reported a large lexical boost effect at lag 0, but crucially, the boost disappeared after lag 0. Abstract priming persisted and was still there at lag 6, independent of modality.

The connection between priming and learning has since been implemented in many different computational models (Chang, 2002; Chang, 2009;

Chang et al., 2000; Chang, Dell, & Bock, 2006; Chang, Janciauskas, & Fitz, 2012; Dell & Chang, 2014; see also Jaeger & Snider, 2013; Reitter, Keller, & Moore, 2011, among others).

Chang and colleagues were the first to model structural priming using a type of neural network model called a simple recurrent network (Chang et al., 2000; 2006; for a useful overview tying together comprehension, production, priming and learning, see Dell & Chang, 2014). The distinctive property of recurrent networks is that they can be trained to learn sequential patterns, hence the idea that they could be suited to learn how to produce sequences of words. In neural networks, information is represented in a distributed fashion over series of interconnected nodes arranged into layers (e.g., an input layer, an output layer, and one or more intermediate or "hidden" layers). Each node (the digital analog of a biological neuron) is capable of receiving and sending numerical signals or *activation* according to a mathematical function, and activation is said to spread throughout the network. The input activation to each node is a mathematical combination of the activation levels of the nodes connected to it from the previous layer. The output activation of a node is computed based on the combination of its input activations and the type of activation function. How the network behaves depends on the numerical strength of the connections or *weights* between nodes. Recurrent neural networks that are trained to learn sequential patterns use information about their prior state to make predictions about each upcoming element. The comparison between what the model predicts and what it observes (either in the initial training set, or in the prime) generates a *prediction error signal* that the model then uses to adjust its connection weights so that its future predictions are more accurate. This is known as *backpropagation*, or *error-driven learning*. Learning via weight changes, however, does not happen instantaneously; therefore, error driven learning cannot account for immediate priming effects, but it can account for overall priming during the course of an entire experiment.

Chang and colleagues (2000)'s recurrent neural network model was built and trained, using error-driven learning, to produce novel English sentences corresponding to transitive, dative, and locative messages. The model had separate components for lexical and for structural processing, so it is referred to as a *dual-path model*. The message layer represented the meanings of transitive, dative, and locative structures, using event semantic representations. The output layer (called the *sequencing layer*) specified both hierarchical and linear constituent orders. The model was trained to map messages onto sequences of words, one word at a time, according to the rules of English, so the model output was a sequence of words with the correct word order for the message. The same model and the same mechanism were then employed to simulate all known behavioral priming effects at the time, including priming when the prime and the target were separated by filler trials, as in the study by Bock and Griffin (2000). To simulate priming, the model was set to produce a prime structure (or sequence, in the model) with error-based learning "on." Over trials, this led to weight changes throughout the network, biasing the system to produce a similar structure to the one presented in the prime. Because weight-changes happen gradually, immediate effects such as priming at lag 0 and the lexical boost cannot be accounted for via changes in the connection weights between message-level representations and the sequencing level, so another mechanism is required to account for immediate priming effects. In another version of the model, Chang and colleagues (2006) proposed that immediate priming effects are due to an explicit memory trace of the prime sentence. The lexical boost effect was explained with a cue-based retrieval mechanism whereby the repeated lexical element (e.g., the verb) acts as cue for the retrieval of the verbatim prime sentence (Bock & Griffin, 2000; Chang et al., 2006; see also Hartsuiker et al., 2008).

A consequence of connecting priming to learning is the prediction that we should observe *inverse preference effects*. The reason is that less expected primes will generate a larger error signal, and hence a larger weight adjustment (and greater learning). This could explain why across many studies less frequent structures, such as passives, show larger priming effects than actives, and why encountering a biased-verb in a dis-preferred argument structure also primes more (Bernolet & Hartsuiker, 2010; Jaeger & Snider, 2008; 2013).

A more recent and updated computational model (Chang et al., 2012) provides a learning account for both short-term and long-term priming, but with a different time-course, hypothetically supported by different memory systems: one fast system relying on explicit (declarative) learning and one slow system relying on implicit (nondeclarative) learning.

The activation-based model introduced by Pickering and Branigan (1998) to account for the lexical boost could not account for long-lasting priming because it had no memory component; however, it is possible to add memory and learning components. Malhotra and colleagues (2008) did this by implementing an activation-model with additional learning and short- and long-term memory components. This dynamic-activation model captures immediate and long-term abstract priming, as well as lexically boosted immediate priming. Along similar lines, Reitter and colleagues (2011) proposed a neural network model to account for both immediate abstract priming and the lexical boost via spreading activation. Lexical boost effects are accounted for via normal spreading activation. Structural representations (e.g., the passive) in this model are themselves represented in long-term memory with a base level of activation. Retrieval of a structure from memory results in a long-term change to its base level of activation, resulting in persistent and cumulative effects.

In addition to predicting relatively long-lived and cumulative effects during the course of an experimental setting, an interesting and important question is whether these effects persist outside of the priming study itself. In a series of experiments aimed at testing the predictions that priming is learning, Kaschak and colleagues (Coyle & Kaschak, 2008; Kaschak, 2007; Kaschak & Borregine, 2008; Kaschak, Kutta, & Schatschneider, 2011, Kaschak, Kutta, & Coyle, 2014; Kaschak, Loney, & Borreggine, 2006) tested whether priming effects would also persist and generalize outside of a priming intervention study and whether inverse preference effects would be observed, with greater priming for less frequent structures, as assessed during a baseline phase.

In Kashak's (2007) and Kashak and colleagues' (2011) studies, priming was cumulative in that concentrated input was given for one structure only. The priming phase was preceded and followed by baseline and post-priming phases to examine changes immediately after priming (Kaschak, 2007) and one week after the experiment (Kaschak et al., 2011). In the baseline phase, participants provided base rates for PO and DO datives in a fragment completion task similar to Pickering and Branigan's (1998). The baseline task served to confirm that DO datives for English speakers are more frequent than POs. During the priming phase, participants received cumulative blocked priming with either one or the other structure: they either completed a block of sentence fragments that either induced POs or DOs. Priming effects were found to be larger for the less frequent structure (PO) confirming the inverse frequency effect. Lasting effects were found immediately post-priming (Kaschak, 2007) and up to one week after the priming intervention phase (Kaschak et al., 2011).

Another line of inquiry into whether there is an implicit learning component to priming examines priming in clinical populations with deficits in explicit memory, but intact implicit memory abilities, as assessed via neuropsychological tests (Ferreira et al., 2008; Heyselaar et al., 2017). Ferreira and colleagues (2008), and more recently Heyselar and colleagues (2021), tested participants with anterograde amnesia. People with this condition are impaired in their ability to form (and consequently, to recall) new memories. At the same time, they are still capable of learning some skills implicitly, such as mirror-reading (Cohen & Squire, 1980). In both Ferreira and colleagues' (2008), and Heyselar and colleagues' (2021) studies, participants with anterograde amnesia showed intact abstract priming effects, in the face of an impaired ability in recognizing previously encountered filler items.

Priming has also been investigated in older adults whose different memory systems are susceptible to differential decline (Heyselar, Wheeldon, &

Segaert, 2021). In a cross-sectional study with participants aged between twenty and eighty-five years, Heyselaar and colleagues (2021) found that short-term abstract priming did not change with age, but that long-term, cumulative priming (i.e., the tendency to increasingly produce a primed structure over the course of the experiment, irrespective of whether it is immediately primed) did. Older adults were more likely to produce primed structures if they had already produced them during the experiment.

Heyselaar and colleagues (2021) propose that different components of nondeclarative memory underly both short-term and long-term structural priming. They account for short-term priming via residual activation, along the lines of Malholtra and colleagues (2008) and Reitter and colleagues (2011), but with the difference that the representations are part of implicit, not explicit memory for the prime.

In conclusion, there is general consensus that a multi-faceted account of structural priming is needed in which a short-term component, responsible for the lexical boost, operates along with a longer-term lexically independent mechanism. On many accounts, abstract priming is understood as a form of implicit learning. The view that abstract priming reflects implicit learning has consequences for how we view language use throughout the lifespan: speakers constantly adapt, or tune their language to the input they receive, in some sense, they never stop learning language (Chang et al., 2000; 2006; Dell & Chang, 2014).

3 Structural Priming in First Language Acquisition

In Section 2, we examined how structural priming paradigms were developed and applied to study grammatical encoding in adult speakers. At the beginning of the 2000s, researchers became interested in exploiting the potential of priming as a tool to investigate linguistic representations in young children, and to use priming to see how children acquire challenging structures like the passive.

A second line of inquiry derived from testing the predictions of implicit learning accounts and comparing the time-course of lexically boosted and abstract priming in children and adults, looking at the effect of moderator variables such as child age, language experience, language proficiency, and measures of working memory.

We will proceed like we did in Section 1 for adults, first addressing the application of priming to the investigation representational questions, then turning to changes over cognitive and linguistic development and the question of longer-lasting priming in children.

3.1 Priming to Investigate Children's Early Sentence Representations

Priming has contributed to an important debate in first language acquisition concerning the abstractness of children's early sentence representations. One view is that children start out combining words with item-specific representations – their early multi-word utterances are assumed to be organized around specific words (e.g., "eat", but not the category "verb") or stored sequences of words (e.g., "eat it", but not "Verb-Noun") (Tomasello, 1992; 2000a; 2000b; 2003). Syntactic abstractions are assumed to emerge gradually, drawing on individual experiences with particular lexical items. On other accounts (e.g., Fisher, 2002; Fisher et al., 2010; Gertner, Fisher, & Eisengart, 2006; Valian, 1986), children's early lexical and syntactic representations are abstract from the beginning of combinatorial language. Children are assumed to have access to lemmas with all of the relevant grammatical information. This is where abstract structural priming paradigms comes in.

Applying the priming logic (see Section 1), if abstract priming is found in a child's production, then the inference is supported that the child has sufficiently abstract phrasal or sentence-level representations to support this kind of priming. Abstract priming is therefore a stringent test for representational abstraction.

Using priming with young children requires taking into consideration children's developing cognitive abilities (in particular working memory, attention, inhibitory control) and their developing language production system (McKee, McDaniel, & Garrett, 2018). Young children have less practice coordinating all of the different processes required to comprehend and speak (for a discussion, see Valian, 2016). Working memory (WM) capacity, attention, and inhibitory control develop with age, and these functions are required to select lemmas among competitors, keep lemmas active at the right stage of sentence formulation, and provide precision timing when inserting lemmas into their appropriate positions (Dell, Oppenheim, & Kittredge, 2008). Whereas there is evidence that children's overall sentence production system is organized qualitatively like the adult system (for an overview, see McKee McDaniel, & Garrett, 2018), lexical access is more challenging for young children (McKee, McDaniel, & Garrett, 2018). Accordingly, priming studies with children often include a familiarization phase to facilitate lexical access, priming sentences are presented with accompanying pictures, the number of fillers is reduced, and in some cases between-subjects designs are employed.

The first study to use a structural priming paradigm with young children, was conducted by Savage and colleagues (2003). They examined abstract and lexically boosted priming for transitives (actives and passives) in English-speaking three- to six-year-olds. The study was presented as a turn-taking game between a live experimenter and the child. Agents and themes in both primes (3.1a–3.1d) and targets (3.1e–3.1h) were always inanimate. In addition to primes with no lexical overlap with the target (3.1a, 3.1b) to test abstract priming, there were primes that contained the pronoun *it* used both for the agent and the patient (3.1c, 3.1d). Under the hypothesis that children's early sentences first develop around high-frequency templates, or "islands" such as "*it*'s verb-ing", "*it*'verb-ed", the idea was that prior to developing a more abstract representation, children would use the template from the prime "*it* is verb-ing *it*". Savage and colleagues (2003) found abstract priming only in six-year-olds. Younger children showed priming only in the conditions with pronouns in the prime (3.1c, 3.1d), which resulted in targets produced with pronouns (3.1e, 3.1f).

(3.1)   PRIMES
      a. The digger pushed the bricks
      b. The bricks got pushed by the digger
      c. It is pushing it
      d. It got pushed by it

      TARGETS
      e. It is breaking it
      f. It got broken by it
      g. The hammer broke the vase
      h. The vase got broken by the hammer

On the basis of these results Savage and colleagues proposed that three- to four-year-olds lack abstract sentence representations. They also proposed an influential developmental model, according to which children's early sentences are either lexically specific or organized around high-frequency templates ("islands") and learning occurs through a gradual process of abstraction over these templates.

Another study, however, found earlier abstract priming for nominal phrases with a prenominal modifier (3.2a) and post-nominal relative clause structure (RC) (3.2b). Branigan, McLean, and Jones (2005) developed a game-version of the priming paradigm adapting the popular British children's game "Snap." The child and the experimenter each have a stack of cards in front of them, and take turns turning over the cards and describing them, looking for matching pairs of cards. When cards match, the first player to shout out "Snap" wins the cards in play. The game continues till one player has won all of the cards. Using this technique with three- to four-year-olds, Branigan and colleagues (2005) found both abstract priming (3.2c and 3.2d primed 3.2e and 3.2f) and a lexical boost effect, meaning that priming was larger when the head noun in the prime (cat) appeared again in the target card (3.2a and 3.2b primed 3.2e and 3.2f, more than 3.2c and 3.2d did).

(3.2)   PRIMES
        a. The blue cat
        b. The cat that is blue
        c. The red dog
        d. The dog that is red

       TARGETS
        e. The green cat
        f. The cat that is green

Huttenlocher, Vasilyeva, and Shimpi (2004) also used structural priming to address the question of abstractness in children's early sentences. They tested four- to five-year-olds using transitive and dative primes, with a task and materials similar to those in Savage and colleagues (2003). Huttenlocher and colleagues (2004), additionally, compared production-to-production priming (Experiment 1: children repeated the prime) to comprehension-to-production priming (Experiment 2: children listened to, but did not repeat the prime). In Experiment 1, children aged 4;5–4;8 (mean 4;8) showed significant priming effects for both transitive and dative trials. In Experiment 2, children aged 4;2–5,7 (mean 4;5) also showed abstract priming effects. Cross-experiment comparisons showed that prime repetition did not make a difference for priming in this age group. In a third experiment with four- to five-year-olds (4;1–5;7, mean 5;3), all of the priming sentences were presented consecutively, in a priming block, followed by a later target block where it was the child's turn to describe all of the targets without any additional input from the experimenter. Again, they found significant priming for both transitive and dative structures, suggesting a longer lasting effect of the prime beyond immediate (0 lag) priming in children. Shimpi and colleagues (2007) tested priming of transitive and dative sentences in a younger group of English-speaking children. They tested three- to four-year-olds, using different variations of the priming procedure: blocked (as in Huttenlocher et al., 2004, Experiment 3) and alternating prime-target trials with repetition of the prime (as in Huttenlocher et al., 2004, Experiment 1). For the blocked version of the experiment, where the target block was presented after the priming block, they found significant structural priming only for the four-year-olds, but not for the three-year-olds. For the version where primes and targets alternate, three-year-olds (2;6–3;5, mean 3;2) showed abstract priming for both datives and transitives.

Taken together, Huttenlocher and colleagues (2004) and Shimpi and colleagues (2007) provide evidence that abstract priming for transitives and datives is robust in four-year-olds and occurs with or without sentence repetition. In younger children, specifically three-year-olds, abstract priming occurs only when children also repeat the prime. One aspect that leads to qualifying these results, somewhat, concerns the scoring criteria used: Huttenlocher and colleagues (2004) and Shimpi and colleagues (2007) used lax scoring criteria and counted as actives sentences with unexpressed objects (e.g., "the truck is dumping mud") and counted as passives truncated passives (e.g., "the truck got hit").

Bencini and Valian (2008) tested abstract priming with transitives in three-year-olds (range 2;11–3;6, mean 3;2) using both strict and lax scoring criteria. Bencini and Valian (2008) developed different scoring schemes as to what counted as an active or a passive. Lax scoring for passives included truncated passives, passives with uninflected verbs, and passives with incorrect inflections. For example, "the ice cream is melt by the sun" and "the ice cream is melting from the sun" were scored as *other* in the strict scoring scheme, but *passive* according to lax scoring. The results showed significant priming effects for both actives and passives, using both strict and lax scoring criteria. When considering lax scoring (but not strict), priming accumulated over trials, with greater priming in the second than the first half of the experiment, consistent with learning over trials.

From the point of view of error-driven learning, it is interesting to note that lax scoring captured those gradient descriptions on a similarity cline with the model presented in the prime. For example, both sentences "the icecream is melt by the sun" and "the icream is melting from the sun" have many of the structural elements of the passive (they are correct at the level of functional processing). What is missing or is incorrect are elements required at the positional level.

Foltz and colleagues (2014) was the first priming study to attempt to relate priming effects to WM capacity. They primed nominal phrases with prenominal modifiers and RC structures, with and without lexical overlap (c.f. Branigan et al., 2005, reviewed earlier) in a group of German-speaking typically developing children (range 4;2–5;7, mean 4;10) and in a group of children with language impairment (range 4;0–5;9, mean 5;10). They also included both lax and strict scoring criteria to also include non-adult attempts at producing primed structures. WM was assessed by having children repeat sequences of numbers of increasing length. They found large priming effects for both groups of children, but neither group exhibited a lexical boost (contrary to Branigan et al., 2005). Importantly, they found a positive relation between working memory and the production of more complex RC structures, and interpreted this result as evidence that sequence memory is particularly relevant to structural priming.

In another study relating structural priming in young children to their WM, Foltz and colleagues (2020) used priming to test the abstractness of sentence representations in children before the age of three (range 2;7–2;11). This study provides the strongest evidence for abstract priming before age three, to date. Foltz and colleagues tested three groups of German speaking two-year-olds. Targets were embedded in a question-answering game with a repeated lead-in (*What is Emma doing? Emma is.*). Children did not repeat primes. Children also provided phonological working memory measures (assessed with a nonword repetition task) and sentence production measures from a developmental language assessment battery. The priming task used infinitive transitives (3.3a) and infinitive intransitives (3.3b). One group of "older" two-year olds (range 2;7–2;11, mean 2;9) participated in a priming study where primes were immediately followed by targets (alternating prime-targets). Two additional groups of "younger" two-year-olds (range for both groups: 2;0–2;6, mean 2;3) were primed with either alternating or blocked primes. Children started with a baseline phase where they provided answers to the lead-in question without a prime. Results showed reliable priming from infinitive transitive primes to infinitive transitive targets compared with infinitive intransitive primes, only for the older group of two-year-olds. For this group, higher sentence production scores were positively related to increased production of infinitive transitive sentences when primed with infinitive transitives. In addition, WM scores were positively related to the primed production of infinitive transitives, but the strength of this effect decreased with age.

(3.3)   a. Baby kitzeln (INFINITIVE TRANSITIVE)
           [baby to tickle/baby tickling]
      b. Laufen (INFINITIVE INTRANSITIVE)
           [to run/running]

In summary, structural priming paradigms and the priming logic have been successfully applied to address highly debated representational questions in first language acquisition. Finding abstract priming – that is, when primes and targets do not share lexical content – at a given age, argues against representations being lexically specific at that age.

3.2 Priming to Investigate Developmental Trajectories in Child Syntax: The Case of Passives

Priming studies in children have contributed empirical data to address the question of why certain structures, such as the passive, are acquired later than related structures, such as actives. It has been proposed (e.g., Borer & Wexler, 1987; 1992; Fox & Grodzinsky, 1998; for a review, see Deen, 2011) that late mastery of the passive derives from maturational constraints on grammatical representations and computations. As we saw in Section 3.1, however, in structural priming studies children produce passives much earlier than in spontaneous speech. If under priming conditions children produce passives, this suggests that a lack of passives in spontaneous speech cannot be imputed to immature grammars. This also shows that priming paradigms are well suited to disentangle whether the late appearance of certain forms in children's speech are due to maturational constraints in their grammars, or other constrains such as developing processing abilities, attention, working memory, and so on.

Several studies have used priming to track the developmental trajectories for passives in three- to four-year-olds and six- to nine-year-olds, focusing on representational questions with respect to the semantics of the passive (Messenger, Branigan, & McLean, 2011; Messenger et al., 2012) and on the question of whether the formal aspects of passives are acquired earlier than the form-meaning mappings (Messenger, Branigan, & McLean, 2012). Messenger and colleagues (2011) found that short (truncated) passive primes (3.4a) primed full passive targets (3.4c) in three- to four-year-olds (range 3;4–4;10, mean 4;1). These results suggest that three- to four-year-old English-speaking children already have a generalized representation for the passive that includes both its full and truncated versions.

(3.4)   PRIMES
         a. The girls are being shocked (SHORT PASSIVE)
         b. The sheep shocking the girl (ACTIVE)

         TARGET
         c. The king is getting scratched by the tiger (FULL PASSIVE)

Messenger and colleagues (2012) manipulated the semantic roles in the primes so as to either be identical to those in the target, or to be different. Targets were always pictures of actional verbs (e.g., *scratch, kick. push*). In the first experiment, they used prime sentences and pictures with actional verbs and AGENT/ PATIENT thematic roles (3.5a, 3.5b) and primes with non-actional verbs (e.g., *shock, scare, surprise*) and theme/experiencer roles (3.5c, 3.5d). They found that English three- to four-year-olds (3;1–4;11, mean 4;2) were equally primed and produced passives both when thematic roles strictly matched across prime and target and when they did not match.

(3.5)   PRIMES
         a. A cow is chasing a witch (ACTIVE, AGENT-SUBJECT, PATIENT-OBJECT)
         b. A witch is being chased by a cow (PASSIVE, PATIENT-SUBJECT, AGENT-
            OBLIQUE)
         c. A sheep is shocking a girl (ACTIVE, THEME-SUBJECT, EXPERIENCER-
            OBJECT)
         d. A girl is being shocked by a sheep (PASSIVE, EXPERIENCER-SUBJECT,
            THEME-OBLIQUE)

         TARGET
         e. A tiger is scratching a king (ACTIVE, AGENT-SUBJECT, PATIENT-OBJECT)

In a second experiment with three- to four-year-olds (3;4–4;11, mean 4;2), they compared priming from theme/experiencer (3.6a, 3.6b) with priming from experiencer/theme primes (3.6c, 3.6d) and found that they equally primed passives in agent/patient targets.

(3.6)   PRIMES
   a.   A sheep is shocking a girl (ACTIVE, THEME-SUBJECT, EXPERIENCER-OBJECT)
   b.   A girl is being shocked by a sheep (PASSIVE, EXPERIENCER-SUBJECT, THEME-OBLIQUE)
   c.   A sheep is loving a girl (ACTIVE, EXPERIENCER-SUBJECT, THEME-OBJECT)
   d.   A girl is being loved by a sheep (PASSIVE, THEME-SUBJECT, EXPERIENCER-OBLIQUE)

   TARGETS
   e.   A tiger is scratching a king (ACTIVE, AGENT-SUBJECT, PATIENT-OBJECT)
   f.   A king is being scratched by a tiger (PASSIVE, PATIENT-SUBJECT, AGENT-OBLIQUE)

These findings show that priming children's passives is not restricted to an overlap in narrow semantic roles and argue against the view that children's early passives are limited agent/patient (actional) verbs.

Children produce passives under priming conditions, but why do they fail to do so in spontaneous speech? Why do they produce more errors than adults, and why do they seem to get the syntax of passives right before passive semantics? Priming studies can help eliminate explanations that appeal to children's immature grammatical systems and point towards processing accounts (Bencini & Valian, 2008).

Messenger, Branigan, and McLean (2012) examined the priming of passives in a group of six-year-olds, (range 6;2–6;11, mean 6;7) and a group of nine-year-olds (range 8;8–10;0, mean 9;6) and found that one common developmental error with passives, reverse role errors (saying: *The dog is chased by the cat*, instead of *The cat is chased by the dog*), occurred frequently in six-year-olds and decreased with age. Reverse role errors were also reported in Bencini and Valian's (2008) study in three-year-olds (these errors were excluded from strict scoring, but included in lax scoring). The reason why children may produce more reverse role errors in priming studies (i.e., "getting the meaning wrong while getting the syntax right") has a likely explanation in the development of working memory and inhibitory control mechanisms.

Tracking the development of the utterances that children produce under priming conditions from earlier ages might be revealing of developmental trajectories themselves (what elements of a complex construction are harder or easier to acquire) and inform theories of priming as learning.

3.3 The Time-Course of Lexically Boosted and Abstract Priming in L1 Acquisition

Priming as learning makes a number of predictions concerning the time-course of the lexical boost and abstract priming in both children and adults. Like some of the studies with adults (e.g., Kaschak, 2007; Kaschak, 2011), longer-lasting priming effects have been found with children aged four-to-five.

Huttenlocher and colleagues (2004; see Section 3.1) found priming effects for datives and passives following a priming block with either passive or dative primes, and Savage and colleagues (2006) found priming for passives following a block of passive primes. These effects persisted one week after priming and one month after priming for the group of children who had also been tested again at one week after the priming intervention. In a pretest posttest blocked design with passives, Kidd (2012) found sustained production of passives at higher rates compared to the pretest.

A few studies have compared the time-course of the lexical boost and abstract priming employing a lag manipulation and also testing both children and adults with the same materials and tasks. These studies are generally consistent with priming as learning: lexically boosted priming is either absent at the youngest ages (Chang et al., 2012) or decays rapidly. Abstract priming effects last over a lag 2 manipulation (Branigan & McLean, 2016) and extend beyond the immediate experiment itself (Messenger, 2021). The prediction that priming should be larger in young children than in adults, however, has not yet been confirmed (Messenger, 2021).

Chang and colleagues (2012) tested three- to four-year-olds, five- to six-year-olds, and adults in a computerized description task, in which participants heard prime sentences describing short video animations of transitive events and produced descriptions of similar target events. They included a lexical manipulation (same/different verb). They found a large lexical boost effect in adults, a smaller lexical boost in the five- to six-year-old group, and no lexical boost in the youngest group. Importantly, they found equivalent (albeit small) abstract priming effects across all the age groups. These results appear to be consistent with an account of the lexical boost that relies on an explicit memory trace for the prime sentence, along with the assumption that explicit memory for sentences develops with age.

In the interactive snap-card game version of priming, Branigan and McLean (2016) tested English-speaking three-and-a-half to five-year-olds and adults. In addition to a lexical overlap manipulation, there was also a lag manipulation (lag 0 and lag 2) to measure the time course of priming effects. Priming effects in children were large (25%), as was the lexical boost effect (an additional 20%) for immediate priming (lag 0). There were no age effects in children. The lexical boost decayed rapidly at lag 2 (a 3% boost), but the abstract priming effect persisted (15%). This overall pattern of effects did not differ significantly from that found in adults. Consistent with the view that priming is learning, children also showed cumulative priming over trials for passives when considering lax scoring criteria, but not with strict scoring (similar to Bencini & Valian, 2008). There was no evidence of cumulative effects for adults.

Messenger (2021) examined short-term and longer-term priming outside of the priming task itself, in children (age range 3;3–4;10, mean age 4;2) and in adults. The study targeted transitive priming, specifically focusing on passives. The study also included a control group, both for the children and the adults. Control groups provided baseline measures for passive production. The priming phase employed the snap-game-technique introduced in Section 3.1, with half of the experimenter's cards on the prime trials presented in the active and half in the passive. The experiment also included immediate and delayed test conditions, assigned between groups. For the immediate group, the experimenter and the participant simply continued to play the snap-game. The participant's cards were still transitive events, but crucially, the experimenter's cards and descriptions were not, so, no additional priming with passives (or actives) was provided. The delayed test condition used the same strategy (i.e., participants were no longer primed with passives). The delayed test condition simply followed another activity (a lexical repetition task). As expected, there were priming effects during the priming phase. In addition, children who had participated in the priming session with actives and passives produced more passives post-priming than children assigned to the baseline condition in which they received no priming. Although Messenger (2021) used both strict and lax scoring schemes, neither the strict nor the lax scoring scheme showed evidence for larger priming in children than adults. Passives were, in fact, extremely rare in children's baseline productions; at baseline and at all phases, adults produced a greater number of passives than children.

Priming magnitude in the absence of lexical repetition has been found to be very variable across studies and across structures, so it remains to be determined whether the predicted larger priming effect will show up in children. One possibility is that during the test phase where children listened to intransitive sentences, these sentences in fact acted as primes for simpler sentence structures than passives. The developmental studies reviewed in this section add to the priming studies reviewed in Section 3.1 that report abstract priming effects at the youngest ages.

3.4 Structural Priming in Bilingual Children

The priming logic can be applied to address the question of how early bilingual children represent sentence structures in their two languages, in a variant of the paradigm known as crosslinguistic priming, in which primes are presented in one language and targets are elicited in the other language. Applying the priming logic crosslinguistically, if one or more structures prime across languages, they are recognized as similar by the bilingual mind. The very first crosslinguistic priming study was conducted with adults (Bock & Loebell, 2003) and most crosslinguistic priming studies to date concentrate on adults; there are only a handful of bilingual priming studies focus on children. Notably, priming studies with adult bilinguals overwhelmingly look at adults who have acquired a second language after acquiring their first one (sequential, or late bilinguals).

In the first crosslinguistic priming study with bilingual children Vasilyeva and colleagues (2010) examined crosslinguistic priming bi-directionally (from English to Spanish and Spanish to English) in bilingual five-to-six-year-olds (range 5;2–6;5, mean 5;11). Although the children were exposed to both languages, they were unbalanced, early bilinguals, with Spanish as their dominant language. They used a between-subjects design both for priming direction (English–Spanish, Spanish–English) and prime condition (active, passive), so that for a given child, priming was concentrated on one structure.

(3.6) PRIMES (SPANISH-TO-ENGLISH)
    a. La pelota rompió la ventana
      [The ball broke the window]
    b. La ventana fue rota par la pelota
      [The window was broken by the ball]

    TARGETS
    a. The dog was washed by the cat
    b. The cat washed the dog

They found reliable priming from Spanish passive primes (3.6b) to English passives (3.6d) but not from English to Spanish. The authors explained the lack of a priming effect from English to Spanish by appealing to differences in frequency and usage between passives in the two languages.

In a more recent follow-up to this initial study, Gámez and Vasilyeva (2020) tested balanced early bilingual six-year-old children, and found bi-directional priming for passives (Spanish to English and English to Spanish). The study also included a verb repetition condition and interestingly, they failed to find a lexical-boost effect.

In the context of the debate concerning the abstraction of children's sentence representations, the crosslinguistic priming data in early bilinguals provide supporting evidence for abstraction, as crucially, primes and targets in different languages do not share words.

3.5 Section Summary

Structural priming studies with young children have contributed crucial empirical data to our current understanding of first language development. In general, priming paradigms provide a useful technique to examine children's grammatical competence while controlling for processing demands associated with lexical retrieval. Priming studies across development have also contributed to our understanding of priming itself. Priming as learning predicts larger effects in less proficient speakers.

Although it is not always possible to compare child priming and adult priming directly because of differences in scoring criteria across labs, some studies show that children exhibit abstract priming before they show lexically boosted priming. In a few studies that adopt lax scoring schemes in addition to strict ones, lax scoring has allowed to detect cumulative effects of priming in children.

Another promising, but still methodologically challenging area of investigation, concerns the relationship between priming and other measures of linguistic and socio-cognitive development.

4 Structural Priming in Second Language Acquisition and Bilingualism

As seen in the previous section, structural priming studies with bilingual children have examined simultaneous bilinguals – that is, children learning both languages at the same time. Priming studies in adult bilinguals, instead, have almost exclusively focused on sequential bilinguals, or second language learners (i.e., speakers who have acquired a second language through formal instruction in a school setting). Following the terminology used in the psycholinguistics literature on priming, unless indicated otherwise, we will use the term bilingual to describe this entire population, L1 to indicate the language acquired first, and L2 the later acquired language.

Structural priming research in adult bilinguals has taken three main strands: the first strand addresses theoretical questions about bilingual language representation and processing; the second examines priming and second language learning, specifically, whether priming occurs in second language learners and whether the effects of priming persist even outside of the priming task; and the third strand uses priming to track developmental changes in learning an L2. Although there are a few studies that have applied priming to child learners of an L2, most studies have addressed adults.

4.1 Priming to Investigate Sentence Representations in Late Bilinguals

Two main hypotheses concerning how bilingual (or multilingual) speakers represent the syntax of a later acquired language are typically contrasted in the bilingual priming literature: a *Separate-Syntax Separate Production System* account (De Bot, 1992), according to which highly proficient bilinguals represent and processes lexical and syntactic structures separately, and a *Shared-Syntax/Shared Grammatical Encoding System* account (Hartsuiker, Pickering, & Veltkamp, 2004), according to which late bilinguals eventually integrate representations for similar syntactic constructions into one shared language-independent representation. For dissimilar constructions, representations are kept language-specific, and separate.

Experiments that employ crosslinguistic priming in both directions (L1 to L2 and L2 to L1) and compare the strength of priming effects across languages to the strength of priming within-languages offer one way to distinguish between different theoretical proposals concerning how multilinguals represent and process syntax in their different languages. If highly proficient multilinguals rely on shared language-independent representations, the prediction is that priming should be equally strong irrespective of priming direction. Additional linguistic variables of interest concern the degree of structural similarity between the two languages, the effects of lexico-semantic similarity in primes and targets (the bilingual equivalent of the lexical boost effect), and the influence of verb bias – that is, whether both languages have the same grammatical encoding options to describe similar events.

The first study to develop the crosslinguistic priming paradigm was Loebell and Bock (2003) who adapted the priming with running recognition memory paradigm to examine crosslinguistic priming of transitives (active, passive) and datives (PO, DO) from English to German. The choice of German and English and active/passive versus DO/PO offers an interesting comparison. DO and PO datives have the same constituent order in both English and German, but actives and passives do not: in German passives, the lexical verb occurs in final position (4.2b). Participants were native speakers of German (L1-German) who had lived in an English-speaking country for at least two years, and who were highly proficient in English (their L2). Loebell and Bock found crosslinguistic priming effects for English and German datives (4.1a, 4.1b) in both directions: DO/PO datives in German primed DO/PO datives in English and vice-versa. For transitives (4.2a, 4.2b), the results were different: there was no crosslinguistic priming for passives. Loebell and Bock explained their results in terms of the need for constituent order to be shared for crosslinguistic priming to occur. They also claim that crosslinguistic priming is explained by implicit learning at the level of the linguistic processes that build utterances. In a far-reaching discussion of the implications of these results they also suggest that crosslinguistic structural priming provides a unified psycholinguistic account of bilingual language use (e.g., code switching, when a linguistic element from language A is inserted into an unfolding utterance in language B) and contact-induced language change.

(4.1) DATIVE PRIMES (GERMAN-TO-ENGLISH/ENGLISH-TO-GERMAN)
   a. Der Musiker verkaufte etwas Kokain an den Agenten/The musician sold some cocaine to the undercover agent/ (PO)
   b. Der Musiker verkaufte dem Agenten etwas Kokain/The musician sold the undercover agent some cocaine/ (DO)

   TARGET
   c. girl, paintbrush, boy, hand (DATIVE PICTURE)

(4.2) TRANSITIVE PRIMES (GERMAN-TO-ENGLISH/ENGLISH-TO-GERMAN)
   a. Eine Gruppe Jugendlicher überfiel den Verkäufer/A gang of teenagers mugged the salesman/ (ACTIVE)
   b. Den Verkäufer wurde von einer Gruppe Jugendlicher überfallen/ The salesman was mugged by a gang of teenagers/ (PASSIVE)

   TARGET
   c. truck, car, tow (TRANSITIVE PICTURE)

Since the seminal study by Loebell and Bock (2003), crosslinguistic structural priming has been found across several pairs of languages. Notably, these language pairs are predominantly Indo-European, and with English as the L2 (English–Spanish, English–Swedish, English–Dutch, English–Chinese, and English–Polish). Although there are studies with other structures, such as genitives and relative clauses, the most frequently primed structures in crosslinguistic research are transitives and datives (Bernolet, Hartsuiker & Pickering, 2007; 2009; 2012; 2013; Cai, Pickering, Yan, & Branigan, 2011; Desmet & Declerp, 2006; Hartsuiker, Pickering, & Veltkamp, 2004; Kantola & van-Gompel, 2011; Salamoura & Williams, 2006; 2007; Schoonbaert, Hartsuiker, & Pickering, 2007; for a reviews, see Hartsuiker & Pickering, 2008; van-Gompel & Arai, 2017).

An influential study by Hartsuiker and colleagues (2004), used crosslinguistic priming to propose a bilingual extension of the lexicalist model of grammatical encoding in language production. Using a dialogue-based priming paradigm with a confederate they tested Spanish–English bilinguals (L1-Spanish, L2-English).

Passive sentence primes were presented in Spanish (4.3a) and were found to prime English passive descriptions to targets pictures (4.3e) compared to active Spanish primes (4.3b). The study also included an intransitive baseline (4.3c) and a constituent fronting construction (LEFT DISLOCATION) (4.3d) in which the object appeared sentence initially (LEFT DISLOCATED OBJECT). The main discourse-function of left dislocation is to topicalize the dislocated constituent. Although, interestingly, left dislocated object primes resulted in numerically more passives than active primes and intransitives, these contrasts were not significant.

(4.3)   PRIMES
    a. El camión es perseguido por el taxi (PASSIVE)
      [The truck is chased by the taxi]
    b. El taxi persigue el camión (ACTIVE)
      [The taxi chases the truck]
    c. El taxi acelera (INTRANSITIVE) [The taxi accelerates]
    d. El camión lo persigue el taxi (LEFT DISLOCATED OBJECT)
      [The truck $_{OBJ}$ (it) chases the taxi $_{SUBJ}$]

    TARGET
    e. missile, boat, hit (TRANSITIVE PICTURE)

The bilingual production model is known as the *shared syntax model*. As mentioned at the beginning of Section 4.1, the model resembles (and is an extension of) the monolingual lexicalist model of sentence production proposed by Pickering and Branigan (1998; see Section 2.1.1). Bilingual structural priming is captured at an abstract level, depending on the structures primed. For priming at the level of argument structure, the model is lexicalist, in that it assumes that it is always mediated by verb lemmas (as in Pickering and Branigan, 1998). Conceptual nodes representing verb-based relational information (e.g., "chase" concept) are connected to language-specific lemmas (e.g., chase [X, Y] in English, perseguir [X, Y] in Spanish). Lemmas are connected to shared category nodes (e.g., verb) and to shared (language independent) combinatorial nodes (active/passive). Lemmas are also connected to general language nodes (e.g., Spanish, English) that act like a switch, controlling what language is being produced.

The prediction of the shared syntax model is that priming effects should be of equal strength within and between the languages of a highly proficient bilingual speaker: L1 to L1, L2 to L1, L2 to L2, and L1 to L2. Some cross-linguistic structural priming studies confirm these predictions, finding equivalent priming from L1-to-L2 and L2-to-L1 (Schoonbaert et al., 2007; Kantola & van Gompel, 2011), and even equivalent priming between additional later acquired languages (L2 and L3) (Hartsuiker et al., 2016), while others do not

(Cai et al., 2011). We will first review studies that have reported equivalent priming.

Schoonbaert and colleagues (2007) reported comparable within-language and between-language priming for datives in L1-Dutch L2-English speakers (4.4). Although there was a numerically greater priming effect within-language, this was not statistically significant. In a subsequent reanalysis of the data from this experiment, Hartsuiker and Bernolet (2016) showed that the difference in priming magnitude found in the earlier study was due to speakers' L2 (English) proficiency. Consistent with the shared syntax model, highly proficient L2-English speakers showed similar abstract priming patterns within their L1 and in their L2, and bi-directionally between the two.

(4.4)   Primes
   a. The cowboy throws the clown a book/De cowboy gooit de clown een boek (DO)
   b. The cowboy throws a book to the clown/De cowboy gooit een boek naar de clown (PO)

    Target picture
   c. Prisoner, apple, pirate, sell

Schoonbaert and colleagues also included a lexical manipulation – called meaning-equivalent condition – where the verb in the prime and in the target are identical in within-language priming, and are translation equivalents in between-language priming. This is shown in 4.5, where primes (4.5a, 4.5b) use translation equivalent verbs – that is, verbs with the same meaning (English *to throw* and Dutch *gooien*) – and in targets 4.5c and 4.5d, where *throw* is used when the target is English, and *gooien* is used when the target is Dutch. When priming from L1-Dutch to L2-English, a meaning-equivalent boost to priming was detected – that is, priming was larger when verbs were translation equivalents (*gooien, throw*) than when they were not (*gooien, sell*, as in 4.4). This semantic-equivalent boost effect was, however, smaller than the well documented within-language verb repetition effect (the classic lexical boost discovered by Pickering and Branigan, 1998, see Section 2.1.2). The results were also asymmetrical. The translation equivalent boost was found going from L1-Dutch to L2-English, but not the other way around. Schoonbaert and colleagues accounted for the asymmetry by assuming that the links between conceptual representations and lemmas in an L2 are weaker than in an L1. Their overall proposal for how bilinguals represent lexical and syntactic information in structures that are similar in their two languages is that lemmas are language-specific, but combinatorial nodes are shared. According to this model, shared conceptual nodes are differentially connected to L1 and L2 lemmas, with stronger concept-to-lemma connections in an L1 than in an L2.

(4.5)   PRIMES
     a. The cowboy throws the clown a book/De cowboy gooit de clown een boek
       (DO SAME VERB/ MEANING EQUIVALENT VERB)
     b. The cowboy throws a book to the clown/De cowboy gooit een boek naar de
       clown (DO SAME VERB/ MEANING EQUIVALENT VERB)

    TARGET PICTURE
     c. Teacher, hat, monk, throw

Consistent with the shared syntax model, equivalent within- (L1 to L1 and L2 to L2) and between-language priming has been found for datives in L1-Swedish L2-English speakers in a written sentence fragment completion priming task (Kantola & van-Gompel, 2011).

In experiments that primed relative clause attachment, Hartsuiker and colleagues (2016) compared within-language priming (L1 to L1) to between-language priming (L1 to L2 and L2 to L1) and to priming between the two later acquired languages (L2 and L3). Note that priming relative clause attachment involves priming at the message level, because primes with different attachment sites have different meanings. So the meaning differences between relative clauses with different attachment sites are greater than the differences between the typical structures used in priming. The first experiment used a fragment-completion priming task and primed relative clause attachments from L1-Dutch, L2-English, and L3-French to L1-Dutch. Two additional experiments crosslinguistically primed relative clause attachment from L1-Dutch to L2-English, and L1-Dutch to L3-French. A fourth experiment used a confederate priming picture description task testing crosslinguistic priming of datives from L1-Dutch, L2-English, and L3-German to L2-English. Across all experiments, priming effects within-language and between-languages were found to be comparable. Finding priming between later acquired languages (an L2 to an L3) suggests that at high levels of proficiency, representations can also be shared across multiple languages. Consistent with this, Facipieri, Vann, and Bencini (2022) found bidirectional crosslinguistic priming (L2-to-L3 and L3-to-L2) for passives with the same task and materials between English L2 and Spanish L3.

Differential priming effects for within- versus between-language priming were, however, reported by Cai and colleagues (2011) with early bilingual adult speakers of Cantonese and Mandarin. Cai and colleagues (2011) also had a cognate verb condition with verbs that are both translation equivalents (as in Schoonbaert et al., 2007) and, additionally, are etymologically related. Although the study by Schoonbaert and colleagues examined priming between languages (English and Dutch), for which many cognates exist, the items chosen for the experiments were overwhelmingly noncognates. Cognates may have a privileged status in a bilingual's mind. For example, Costa, Caramazza and Sebastián-Gálles (2000) found that Catalan–Spanish bilinguals were faster in naming pictures that had cognate names in Catalan and Spanish than pictures with noncognate names. Cai and colleagues (2011) reported a lexical boost effect in within-language priming, and a much smaller between-language cognate boost effect. To account for the within-language versus between-language priming asymmetry, Cai and colleagues (2011) do not reject the overall architecture of shared syntax model, but they propose a more active role for the global language nodes, by assuming that they act exactly like the other nodes in the model. The idea is that the language nodes activate when a specific language is spoken, and this activation spreads to all lemmas of that language, resulting in a within-language boost even in the absence of lexical overlap. Moreover, they speculate that there may also be an inhibitory mechanism at play in accessing shared representations, such that when one language is turned on, the other language may be inhibited. As for the status of cognates, they argue that cognates are represented as separate lemmas, against positions that view cognates as sharing representations.

The shared syntax model, however, is not the only way to capture crosslinguistic priming effects. An alternative model is that speakers have separate but connected representations for similar structures, as proposed recently by Ahn and Ferreira (2024). On this "Separate-but-Connected" account (Ahn & Ferreira, 2024), crosslinguistic structural priming occurs because the structure in one language activates a related, but separate, structure in the other language. The Separate-but-Connected account also predicts smaller between-language priming than within-language priming. The reason is that between-language priming results from the transmission of activation between two separate combinatorial nodes (one for each language), whereas within-language priming results from the residual activation of one combinatorial node.

Another question addressed via priming is whether priming in an L2 depends on whether the bilingual speaker's L1 has that structure or not. At high proficiency levels, L1 experience with a structure in the L1 does not seem to influence within-language priming in an L2. In a within-language priming study for DOs in proficient L2-English speakers, L1-Spanish and L1-German showed equal amounts of priming (Flett, Branigan & Pickering, 2013). But we will address the question of how priming, L1 and L2 characteristics, and prior linguistic experience with a structure interact with proficiency in the following section.

In Section 2.1.4, we addressed the question of whether priming can occur between constructions that are similar at the functional level but differ in constituent order. As was the case for monolingual priming, the evidence is mixed, with some crosslinguistic studies failing to find priming when constituent order differs (Loebell & Bock, 2003; Bernolet et al., 2007) and some finding priming irrespective of constituent order differences (Desmet & Declerq, 2006; Chen, Jia, Wang, Dunlap & Sin, 2013; Shin & Christianson, 2009). Desmet and Declerq (2006) found crosslinguistic priming of relative-clause attachment from Dutch to English, despite differences in constituent order. Chen and colleagues (2013) found bi-directional priming of passives between English and Chinese, again, despite differences in constituent order. In a recent computational model of crosslinguistic priming as implicit learning, Khoe and colleagues (2021) successfully modeled crosslinguistic priming between structures in English and Dutch with different word orders.

Many of the crosslinguistic effects reviewed above can be accounted for nicely by the shared syntax model. This model, however, deals with adult multilinguals who have achieved high levels of proficiency in their L2. Two questions arise with respect to priming and learning a second language: whether priming can in fact also function as an intervention to stimulate language learning, and whether priming effects change across different developmental stages in an L2. We will address each of these issues in the following sections.

4.2 Priming and Second Language Learning

The proposal that priming is an adaptive language-learning mechanism that continues into adulthood (see Section 2.2.2) has sparked an interest in examining whether priming supports L2 learning and extends beyond the priming task itself (for a review, see Jackson, 2018). Again, as noted in Section 2.2.2, use of the terms *long-term* or *long-lasting priming* should be qualified with the modifier "relatively." In monolingual adults and children, long-term priming studies typically examine priming effects over varying intervening distractor trials. These studies have provided data in support of the view that priming is a form of implicit learning, whereby the production system learns to express messages in certain ways in response to input, so it makes sense to ask the same type of questions when adults learn an additional language. Additionally, some priming studies with adult L2 learners have tested whether priming can function as a learning intervention, by also including pre- and post-priming assessments.

The first priming study to test priming as a learning intervention in an L2 context was McDonough (2006), who used the confederate priming paradigm with datives. This study was designed to include a baseline and a post-priming phase, using a picture description task to elicit datives. The priming phase targeted PO and DO datives. Participants were low-proficiency L2 speakers of English. In the priming phase, priming was successful for POs, but not for

DOs. PO production carried over into the post-priming phase, with more PO descriptions produced than in the baseline phase. Another experiment primed DOs only, but again, priming was not significant, and participants produced more POs despite having being primed with DOs. There was, however, an indication that priming itself led to a greater production of DOs. L2 learners who had produced at least one DO at baseline were more likely to produce DOs during priming. McDonough's interpretation of the lack of priming for DOs takes inspiration from L1 priming work that takes lack of evidence for priming as evidence for item-specific representations. McDonough, in fact, suggests that at the early stages of L2 development for DO structures in English, these structures may be tied to specific items, specifically pronouns, because DOs occur more frequently with pronouns in English. Based on these priming results, McDonough proposed an item-specific developmental trajectory for L2 syntax, along the lines of similar proposals in L1 development (e.g., Savage et al., 2003).

In the first within-language L2 priming study that directly considered proficiency as a moderator variable, Kim and McDonough (2008) examined active/passive priming in English L2 with Korean L1 speakers who were grouped into three proficiency groups based on performance on a cloze test. They included a verb overlap condition (same/different verb) and included verbs that varied in the frequency of occurrence in the passive in English, as determined by corpora. Kim and McDonough reported abstract priming and a lexical boost for all three proficiency levels, but the effect size of the lexical boost was larger for the lower-proficiency group.

Another test of priming as implicit learning in an L2 context was conducted by Shin and Christianson (2012). This study is the only study, to my knowledge, that compares the effects of priming with additional explicit grammatical rule instruction embedded in the same experiment, and includes immediate and post-priming assessment phases. Pretest and posttest assessments consisted of a pictured-based sentence production task, with the target structures stimulated in the priming task (POs/DOs and phrasal verb constructions), and a grammaticality judgment task. Pre-tests took place immediately before the priming phase, and the immediate posttest occurred right after. For the long-term test, participants came back to the lab the next day. In the priming phase, L1-Korean L2-English speakers who were proficient in English (and had lived in an English-speaking country for at least three years) were primed with PO/DO datives and separated phrasal verb constructions (*The man is putting the fire out/The man is putting out the fire*). The priming phase included a lag manipulation (lag 0 vs. lag 4–5). At lag 0, there was also an instruction manipulation (explicit instruction, no instruction). In the explicit instruction condition, participants were provided with a grammatical explanation of the rules for DO/POs and particle verb placement in English. All manipulations were between subjects. Shin and Christianson found different effects for DO/POs versus phrasal verbs within the priming phase itself, immediately post-priming, and one day later. All priming conditions (lag 0, with explicit instruction, 0 lag without explicit instruction, and 4–5 lag – which was always without explicit instruction) yielded priming effects within the priming task itself. For DO/POs, explicit instruction at lag 0 resulted in greater priming than priming at lag 0 without explicit instruction, and greater than priming at lag 4–5. For separated phrasal verb constructions, lag 0 priming resulted in equal amounts of priming irrespective of explicit instruction, and these effects were larger than priming over lag 4–5. For DOs, the advantage of explicit instruction persisted in the immediate post-priming production task. For the long-term phase one day later, however, only participants who had received priming over lag 4–5 demonstrated sustained production of DOs, compared to those who had received 0 lag priming and 0 lag priming with explicit instruction. For phrasal verb constructions, effects were similar, independent of priming manipulation and instruction. Shin and Christianson imputed the differential effects of priming manipulation on longer-term maintenance and generalization of target structures to novel items to an interaction between implicit learning and structural complexity. They argued that for more complex structures such as DO datives, compared to phrasal verbs, implicit learning (induced via the lag manipulation) may be optimal for long-term learning.

Priming studies in an L2 setting demonstrate the potential of using priming translationally, as an intervention to support second language learning. One additional attractive feature of the L2 priming studies conducted in the context of second-language learning is that they employ pretest-posttest designs to determine whether priming effects generalize and persist outside of the priming task. Many L2 priming studies confirm that the effects of priming interventions generalize and persist (e.g., McDonough & Mackey, 2008; McDonough & Chaikitmongkol, 2010; McDonough, Trofimovich, & Newman, 2015, Shin & Christianson, 2012), although the question remains as to how exactly these effects are modulated by proficiency, first language properties (e.g., structural similarity), and learner characteristics (for discussion and review of within-language priming in an L2, see Jackson, 2018).

4.3 Priming and Developmental Trajectories in an L2

Priming has increasingly been used to track how late bilinguals, and second language learners' representations change developmentally. This line of inquiry parallels the interest in applying priming to address development of an L1.

Whereas priming studies in L1 development track priming over age, the bulk of the studies that address L2 learning consider the relationship between known priming effects, such as the lexical boost and abstract priming and L2 language proficiency.

A study that directly sets out to use priming to examine developmental trajectories in an L2, including proficiency as a variable, was conducted by Bernolet, Hartsuiker, and Pickering (2013), with L1-Dutch L2-English speakers from the Dutch-speaking region of Belgium (Flanders, adjective Flemish). They aimed to test a developmental model of L2 syntax acquisition by tracking lexically dependent and abstract priming effects over proficiency levels. Across two experiments, they primed genitive constructions from Dutch to English and within English (L2). The English Saxon genitive ('s genitive) is a difficult structure for Flemish learners of English. Although Dutch has a construction that resembles the Saxon genitive in constituent order (possessor/possessed), this structure is not marked morphologically, and it occurs less frequently than the prepositional genitive. In both the between-language experiment (Experiment 1) and the within-language experiment (Experiment 2), possessed objects (e.g., a skateboard) were the same across prime and target for the repeated meaning conditions (4.6a, 4.6b) and different for the different meaning conditions (4.6c, 4.6d). In the same meaning condition, head nouns used to refer to the possessed objects were therefore translation equivalents in the between-language priming experiment and identical in the within-language priming experiment.

(4.6)   PRIMES
      a. The nun's skateboard is blue/De non haar skatebard is blauw (*'s* GENITIVE, SAME)
      b. The skateboard of the nun is blue/Het skatebord van de non is blauw (*of* GENITIVE, SAME)
      c. The nun's bottle is blue/ De non haar papfles is blauw (*'s* GENITIVE, DIFFERENT)
      d. The bottle of the nun is blue/Het papfles van de non is blauw (*of* GENITIVE, DIFFERENT)

      TARGET PICTURE
      e. pirate, blue skateboard

In the between-language priming experiment there was a lexical boost effect (i.e., a translation equivalent boost) and increased abstract priming of *'s* genitives (the dis-preferred structure) as proficiency increased. At the lowest proficiency levels, bilinguals showed no between-language priming. In the within-L2 priming experiment, there was priming for *'s* genitives and a large lexical boost. Importantly, proficiency interacted with priming magnitude and the lexical boost, with different effects for high- versus low-proficiency speakers. Less proficient speakers showed large priming effects in the lexical overlap condition and smaller abstract priming effects. There was a trend towards stronger abstract priming in more proficient speakers. In a combined analysis with both experiments, within-language priming turned out to be stronger than between-language priming. Bernolet and colleagues (2013) proposed a developmental trajectory according to which at lower proficiency levels L2 speakers start out with lexically specific representations and gradually abstract over items. At high levels of proficiency, multilinguals merge their representations for similar structures into one shared representation. On this account, the shared syntax model represents an "end state" for language learning.

A more fleshed out version of developmental model for L2 can be found in Hartsuiker and Bernolet's (2017) study. We can illustrate the developmental stages using the acquisition of the English DO dative as an example. An L2 learner would start out with lemma-specific syntactic representations. For example, an English-L2 learner's initial representation for the verb *give* would be item specific in that it would be connected to the DO argument structure on a verb-specific basis, with no generalization over English verbs that also occur in the DO. Because at the beginning stages of L2 learning there is no abstract representation of the DO, priming relies on L2 speaker's explicit memory for the prime. Lexical overlap acts as a retrieval cue for the prime, thus explaining why at very low proficiency levels L2 speakers exhibit greater lexically dependent priming. With increased proficiency, syntactic representations abstract over verbs that are observed in the DO (e.g., the nodes for various English ditransitive verbs, such as *give* and *show* become connected to a single generalized DO node). At higher proficiency levels bilinguals will also abstract away from language-specific constructions and merge representations on the basis of both structural and semantic-pragmatic similarity.

Although there is some priming evidence that experience with a structure in the L1 does not affect priming magnitude in an L2 in highly proficient speakers (Flett et al., 2013), other priming studies have found that the priming magnitude and longer-term effects of priming depend on interaction between proficiency and a combination of the properties of the L1 and the L2. For example, Kaan and Chun (2018) claim to have found an effect of the frequency of a structure in the L1 when comparing priming of English DOs and POs in monolingual English and L2-English speakers who had Korean as their L1. Both Korean and English have POs and DOs, but whereas DO is more frequent in English, PO is more frequent in Korean. They observed cumulative priming during the experiment (as a function of the number of DOs/POs experienced prior to a given trial) and an inverse preference effect consistent with language biases: native English speakers showed more priming for POs, whereas L2-English speakers showed greater priming for DO. This suggests an influence of L1 experience.

Future studies can exploit the priming paradigm to investigate how priming effects are modulated by proficiency, first language properties (e.g., structural similarity, frequency of the structures), and learner characteristics.

5 Summary and Conclusions

This Element has provided a historic panorama of structural priming research in three different populations of speakers, starting from the origins of this paradigm within the context of psycholinguistic models of sentence production. The success of this paradigm cannot be overstated. Priming studies in adults, children, and second language learners are increasingly used to address representational questions outside of the domain of language production research in linguistics, first and second language acquisition, and bilingualism.

The adult structural priming data reviewed in Section 2 clearly supports a view of the architecture for language where lexical processes are distinct from structural processes, as evidenced by lexically independent structural priming (Section 2.1.1). The data are also consistent with an overall separation of form versus meaning-based priming, as priming studies show that syntactic structure can be primed independent of semantic and information structure, and vice versa (Section 2.1.2). Priming occurs at a level that corresponds to the lemma level in sentence production models, as it is insensitive to morphological structure and metrical structure. Priming, however, has increasingly been shown to cumulative, the more dimensions align (lexical, syntactic, semantic, pragmatic), the greater the priming. This contrasts with early claims that one dimension – syntax – mattered for priming. As a consequence, more recently studies have turned to priming as a way of tapping into semantic structure (Section 2.1.5.3).

In addition to addressing *what* is primed, Section 2 also addresses the research on *why* people are primed. The view that priming is a form alignment in conversation, relying on shared representations at multiple levels of representation and between modalities (comprehension and production) is exciting for psycholinguistics and linguists alike, because it brings closer together representational theories (theories of language knowledge or competence) and theories of language use (performance). It also suggests an avenue for more research into priming at the level of information structure constructions that occur more frequently in dialogue. Implicit learning accounts of priming challenge the view that adult linguistic competence is static. It implies greater linguistic malleability and learning throughout the lifespan, with age-related changes in older adults that are beginning to be explored. We saw that the proposal that abstract priming is learning motivated a lot of the literature that compares priming in adults with priming in first and second language learners.

In Section 3 we reviewed the contributions of priming research in first language acquisition. An important finding is the fact that children exhibit abstract priming early on, arguing for early abstraction accounts of children's sentence representations. The bulk of the priming studies with children have examined priming where syntax and semantics covaried, so future child priming studies should apply the priming logic more broadly and examine the broader range of questions addressed in the adult priming literature with respect to the relationship between form-based priming and meaning and information structure priming. This will provide a better picture of whether children master certain aspects better than others and how this relates to linguistic and nonlinguistic moderator variables. Studies that have looked at these utterances have revealed more subtle developmental patterns, which can also provide additional data to test error-driven learning accounts of priming. Although structural priming taps into linguistic representations, it is important to keep in mind that priming data are the result of a language processing system, and therefore, should be always interpreted within the context of a sentence production model. This caveat is especially important for studies with young language learners, where, traditionally, researchers have focused more on language competence, and less on language performance.

In Section 4 we saw how studies on within- and between-language structural priming with adult second language speakers have contributed to our understanding of how multilinguals represent and process sentences. The finding that structures can be primed across languages (even in the absence of shared word order) is evidence for the high level of abstraction at which priming operates. Compared to the priming literature with monolingual speakers, crosslinguistic structural priming studies are still restricted to a more limited set of "classic" constructions, such as actives/passives and datives. It is clear that to get a full picture of how priming changes over proficiency levels and how priming results may differ depending on the kind of construction investigated, L2 priming studies should extend the number and types of representations studied. At the same time, priming studies across different populations of speakers now rest on a solid empirical base. Priming paradigms offer a rich tool to investigate many different kinds representational questions in multilinguals, and have the potential of fueling translational research on interventions that support second language learning.

5.1 A Revised Model of Grammatical Encoding

Models of grammatical encoding have tacitly imported an assumption from a long tradition in linguistics that views the main verb as being central to encoding those aspects of meaning that matter to syntax, or how semantics is mapped onto syntax. For example, in Section 2.1.1, we noted that the Pickering and Branigan (1998) lemma model of grammatical encoding is verb-centered and lexicalist: it assumes that grammatical encoding necessarily requires activating a verb lemma, which then activates its combinatorial nodes.

There are reasons to question whether this entirely verb-centered view of sentence representation and sentence production is correct. Linguists working in very different theoretical frameworks (Borer, 2005; Goldberg, 1995; Levin & Rappaport Hovav, 2005; Ramchand, 2008; for a review and discussion, see Marantz, 2013) have observed that verbs appear in a larger set of argument structures (Pickering and Branigan's combinatorial nodes) than typically assumed. Consider a prototypically transitive verb in English: *kick*. 'Kick' in English can occur in at least eight grammatical frames (5.1a–5.1e; examples from Bencini and Goldberg, 2000):

(5.1)
    a. Pat kicked the wall
    b. Pat kicked Bob the football
    c. Pat kicked Bob black and blue
    d. Pat kicked the football into the stadium
    e. Pat kicked at the wall
    f. Pat kicked her foot against the chair
    g. Horses kick
    h. Pat kicked her way out of the operating room

Each one of these occurrences of the verb *kick* in a sentence is an instance of a more general type of event. For example, 5.1b entails transfer: the sentence can be paraphrased as "Pat caused Bob to have the ball by kicking it." On its own, however, the verb kick does not entail transfer (cf. 5.1a, 5.1c, 5.1d, etc.). So where is this component of meaning to be located? This question is at the heart of the debate between lexicalist and constructionist treatments of argument structure. The classic way of dealing with this is to assume different verb senses for each argument structure (e.g., Levin and Rappaport Hovav, 2005; Rappaport Hovav and Levin, 1998; Pinker, 1989), so, on this view, there would, in fact, be multiple senses of the verb *kick*, including a sense that does not entail transfer and one that does. From the point of view of the speaker, this means that there are multiple long-term linguistic representations, each one corresponding to a different sense, and that the speaker selects the correct sense based on the message she/he intended to express. Goldberg (1995) pointed out that the multiple sense view also results in having to stipulate implausible verb senses for many verbs, to account for sentences like the ones in 5.2a–5.2c.

(5.2)   a. The woman sneezed the foam off the cappuccino [*sneeze* sense: X cause Y move Z by sneezing]
         b. The train screeched into the station [*screech* sense: Y moves while screeching]
         c. She saw him into the room [*see* sense: X accompanies Y while moving]

An alternative view is to recognize the existence of verb-independent semantic generalizations directly linked to sentence structures; in other words, to recognize that sentence structures themselves contribute to the interpretation of a sentence. This level of generalization above the verb is captured in *Argument Structure Constructions* (Goldberg, 1995, 2006, for an introduction and application of Construction Grammar to the analysis of English, see Hilpert, 2014; Hoffman, 2022). Constructions are, more broadly, pairings of "form and function" that exist at all levels of generalization (Goldberg, 1995, 2006). Semantically, argument structure constructions encode meanings that are central to human experience and cognition. Goldberg (1995) calls this the "scene-encoding hypothesis" (p. 39). Across languages, it is common to find sentence patterns that encode basic meanings such as experiencing a stimulus, undergoing a change of state, causing a change of state in another entity, transferring an object, moving along a path, and so on. The meaning side of an argument structure construction is expressed using the semantics of event structures (see Section 2.1.5.3). On a constructional approach, a semantic division of labor is posited between the more abstract relational meanings carried by constructions and the more specific meanings carried by verbs (Goldberg, 1995; 2006). For example, in 5.1b, the meaning [X CAUSE Y to HAVE Z] is associated directly with the DO construction, the semantic contribution of the main verb is, in turn, to modify the event by providing the specifics of the means by which the transfer is achieved (i.e., the act of kicking). In the case of the two intransitive verbs *sneeze* and *screech* in 5.2, *sneeze* modifies the X CAUSE Y TO MOVE meaning expressed directly by the English *caused motion construction*, and *sneeze* expresses the means. Similarly, *screech* expresses the manner. The "function side" of a construction encompasses semantics and information structure. On a constructional account, although passives express the same semantic relations as actives, they differ in their information structure, as passives typically serve the discourse function of making the patient more prominent than the agent, and placing it in a topical position (for a constructional analysis of English passives, see Hilpert, 2014).

With this additional representational machinery in the grammar, we are ready to propose a revision of the consensus model of grammatical encoding that captures all of the priming findings in monolingual adults, including the more recent studies that examined the nature of semantic representations, reviewed in Section 2.1.5. The constructional (as opposed to lexicalist) model recognizes the existence of verb-independent mappings from messages to grammatical encoding (Bencini, 2013; 2017; 2020). Figure 7 shows the generation of the sentence *The girl gives her teacher a flower*. In addition to verb-specific participant roles, associated with the core semantics of the verb *give* ("giver", "givee", "given"), the model recognizes the semantic contribution of the event structure X CAUSES Y to HAVE Z associated with the DO construction in English. In this case, the integration of verb and constructional semantics is seamless, as the number of verb-specific roles matches up with the number of argument slots (variables) in the construction. The constructional model also accounts for those cases of "implausible verb senses" in 5.2, when the number of verb participant roles is a subset of the number of argument roles (see Figure 8). To account for the production of *The woman sneezed the foam off the cappuccino*, the intransitive, monovalent predicate *sneeze* has only a participant role (we can call it "the sneezer"). It is the abstract English caused motion construction that contributes the two additional argument roles required and the overall more abstract CAUSE-TO-MOVE interpretation, while the predicate

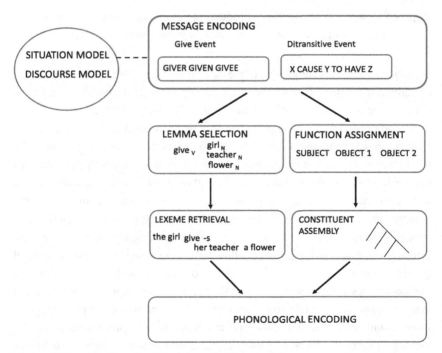

Figure 7 Constructional sentence production model, same number of argument roles in argument structure construction and verb.

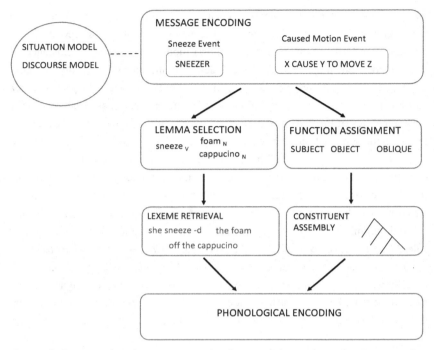

Figure 8 Constructional sentence production model, number of argument roles in argument structure construction is greater than in the verb.

contributes the means component of the event (Goldberg, 1995). The combination of verbs and constructions is by no means an unregulated relationship. I refer the reader to the relevant linguistics literature (e.g., Goldberg, 1995, 2006).

Although constructional approaches vary (see Hoffman and Trousdale 2013; Ungerer and Hartmann, 2023), one key finding is that constructions have the right level of abstraction to account for both for abstract (lexically independent) and for lexically boosted priming and the full range of priming effects reviewed in this Element. By recognizing sentence level form-function mappings, the constructional model means the finding that the more dimensions align (lexical, syntactic, semantic, pragmatic), the greater the priming can be accounted for. Because constructional approaches allow for the existence of intermediate-level generalizations, they make it also possible to account for the results of Ziegler and colleagues (2019), which is a challenge for the notion of purely abstract syntactic priming. The constructional model is consistent with implicit learning models with a dual architecture and event semantic representations for the message (along the lines of Chang et al., 2006) and with more structurally guided models of sentence production (Bock and Ferreira, 2014; Konopka and Bock, 2009; Konopka and Meyer, 2014).

To conclude, there are advantages to adopting a broadly constructional approach to linguistic representation over theoretical frameworks in linguistics that consider constructions to be epiphenomenal. The fact that constructions can be primed provides behavioral evidence that they are active in real-time language use. There is a welcome convergence between linguistic and psycholinguistic approaches that recognize priming as a suitable method to tap into linguistic representations (Bencini, 2002; Bencini, 2013; Bencini, 2020; Branigan, Pickering, Liversedge, Stewart, & Urbach, 1995; Cai & Zhao, 2024; Branigan & Pickering, 2017).

References

Ahn, D., & Ferreira, V. (2024). Shared vs. separate structural representations: Evidence from cumulative cross-language structural priming. *Quarterly Journal of Experimental Psychology, 77*, 174–190.

Baker, M. C. (1988). *Incorporation: A theory of grammatical function changing*. Chicago, IL: University of Chicago Press.

Baker, M. C. (1996). On the structural positions of themes and goals. In J. Rooryck & L. Zaring (Eds.), *Phrase structure and the lexicon* (pp. 7–34). Dordrecht: Springer.

Baker, M. C. (1997). Thematic roles and syntactic structure. In L. Haegeman (Ed.), *Elements of Grammar* (pp. 73–137). Dordrecht: Springer.

Bencini, G. M. L. (2002). The representation and processing of argument structure constructions. Unpublished doctoral dissertation. University of Illinois, Urbana-Champaign.

Bencini, G. M. L. (2013). Psycholinguistics. In T. Hoffmann & G. Trousdale (Eds.), *The Oxford handbook of construction grammar* (pp. 379–396). Oxford: Oxford Academic Press.

Bencini, G. M. L. (2017). Speech errors as a window on language and thought: A cognitive science perspective. *Altre Modernità*, special issue, *Errors: Communication and Its Discontents*, 243–262.

Bencini, G. M. L. (2020). Developing convergence: Towards an integrated developmental model of language representation and processing in children and adults. In Cardinaletti, A., Branchini, C., Giusti, G., & Volpato, F. (Eds.), *Language acquisition, processing and bilingualism: Selected papers from the Romance Turn VII* (pp. 12–46). Cambridge: Cambridge Scholar Publishing.

Bencini, G. M. L., & Goldberg, A. E. (2000). The contribution of argument structure constructions to sentence meaning. *Journal of Memory and Language, 43*, 640–651.

Bencini, G. M. L., & Valian, V. V. (2008). Abstract sentence representations in 3-year-olds: Evidence from language production and comprehension. *Journal of Memory and Language, 59*, 97–113.

Bernolet, S., Colleman, T., & Hartsuiker, R. J. (2014). The 'sense boost' to dative priming: Evidence for sense-specific verb-structure links. *Journal of Memory and Language, 76*, 113–126.

Bernolet, S., Collina, S., & Hartsuiker, R. J. (2016). The persistence of syntactic priming revisited. *Journal of Memory and Language, 91*, 99–116.

Bernolet, S., & Hartsuiker, R. J. (2010). Does verb bias modulate syntactic priming? *Cognition*, *114*, 455–461.

Bernolet, S., Hartsuiker, R. J., & Pickering, M. J. (2007). Shared syntactic representations in bilinguals: Evidence for the role of word-order repetition. *Journal of Experimental Psychology: Learning, Memory, and Cognition*, *33*, 931–949.

Bernolet, S., Hartsuiker, R. J., & Pickering, M. J. (2009). Persistence of emphasis in language production: A cross-linguistic approach. *Cognition*, *112*, 300–317.

Bernolet, S., Hartsuiker, R. J., & Pickering, M. J. (2013). From language-specific to shared syntactic representations: The influence of second language proficiency on syntactic sharing in bilinguals. *Cognition*, *127*, 287–306.

Bock, J. K. (1982). Toward a cognitive psychology of syntax: Information processing contributions to sentence formulation. *Psychological Review*, *89*, 1–47.

Bock, J. K. (1986a). Meaning, sound, and syntax: Lexical priming in sentence production. *Journal of Experimental Psychology: Learning, Memory, and Cognition*, *12*, 575–586.

Bock, J. K. (1986b). Syntactic persistence in language production. *Cognitive Psychology*, *18*, 355–87.

Bock, J. K. (1989). Closed-class immanence in sentence production. *Cognition*, *31*, 163–186.

Bock, J. K. (1995). Sentence production: From mind to mouth. In J. L. Miller & P. D. Eimas (Eds.), *Handbook of perception and cognition: Speech, language, and communication* (vol. 11, pp. 181–216). San Diego: Academic Press.

Bock, J. K., & Ferreira, V. S. (2014). Syntactically speaking. In M. Goldrick, V. S. Ferreira, & M. Miozzo (Eds.), *The Oxford handbook of language production* (pp. 21–46). Oxford: Oxford University Press.

Bock, J. K., & Griffin, Z. M. (2000). The persistence of structural priming: Transient activation or implicit learning? *Journal of Experimental Psychology:General*, *129*, 177–192.

Bock, J. K., & Kroch, A. (1989). The isolability of syntactic processing. In G. N. Carlson & M. K. Tanenhaus (Eds.), *Linguistic structure in language processing* (pp. 157–196). Dordrecht: Kluwer.

Bock, J. K., & Levelt, W. J. (1994). Language production: Grammatical encoding. In M. A. Gernsbacher (Ed.), *Handbook of psycholinguistics* (pp. 945–984). San Diego: Academic Press.

Bock, J. K., & Loebell, H. (1990). Framing sentences. *Cognition*, *35*, 1–39.

Bock, J. K., Loebell, H., & Morey, R. (1992). From conceptual roles to structural relations: Bridging the syntactic cleft. *Psychological Review, 99,* 150–171.

Bock, J. K., Dell, G. S., Chang, F., & Onishi, K. H. (2007). Persistent structural priming from language comprehension to language production. *Cognition, 104,* 437–458.

Borer, H. (2005). *In name only: Structuring sense,* vol. 1. Oxford: Oxford University Press.

Borer, H., & Wexler, K. (1987). The maturation of grammar. In T. Roeper & E. Williams (Eds.), *Parameter setting.* Dordrecht: Reidel.

Borer, H., & Wexler, K. (1992). Bi-unique relations and the maturations of grammatical principles. *Natural Language and Linguistic Theory, 10,* 147–189.

Branigan, H. (2007). Syntactic priming. *Language and Linguistics Compass, 1,* 1–16.

Branigan, H., & Mclean, J. (2016). What children learn from adults' utterances: An ephemeral lexical boost and persistent syntactic priming in adult-child dialogue. *Journal of Memory and Language, 91,* 141–157.

Branigan, H., Mclean, J., & Jones, M. (2005). A blue cat or a cat that is blue? Evidence for abstract syntax in children's noun phrases. In Brugos, A., Clark-Cotton, M. R., & Ha, S. (Eds.), *Proceedings of the 29th Annual Boston University Conference on Language Development* (pp. 109–121), Somerville: Cascadilla Press.

Branigan, H. P., & Pickering, M. J. (2017). An experimental approach to linguistic representation. *The Behavioral and Brain Sciences, 40,* article e282.

Branigan, H. P., Pickering, M. J., & Cleland, A. A. (2000). Syntactic coordination in dialogue. *Cognition, 75,* B13–B25.

Branigan, H. P., Pickering, M. J., Liversedge, S. P., Stewart, A. J., & Urbach, T. P. (1995). Syntactic priming: Investigating the mental representation of language. *Journal of Psycholinguistic Research, 24,* 489–506.

Branigan, H. P., Pickering, M. J., McLean, J. F., & Cleland, A. A. (2007). Syntactic alignment and participant role in dialogue. *Cognition, 104,* 163–197.

Branigan, H. P., Pickering, M. J., Stewart, A. & McLean, J. (2000). Syntactic priming in spoken production: Linguistic and temporal interference. *Memory and Cognition, 28,* 1297–1302.

Bresnan, J., & Kanerva, J. (1989). Locative inversion in Chicheŵa: A case study of factorization in grammar. *Linguistic Inquiry, 20,* 1–50.

Cai, Z. G., Pickering, M. J., Yan, H., & Branigan, H. P. (2011). Lexical and syntactic representations in closely related languages: Evidence from

Cantonese–Mandarin bilinguals. *Journal of Memory and Language, 65,* 431–445.

Cai, Z. G., Pickering, M. J., & Branigan, H. P. (2012). Mapping concepts to syntax: Evidence from structural priming in Mandarin Chinese. *Journal of Memory and Language, 66,* 833–849.

Cai, Z. & Zhao, N. (2024). Structural priming: An experimental paradigm for mapping linguistic representations. *Language and Linguistics Compass, 18,* article e12507. https://doi.org/10.1111/lnc3.12507.

Chang, F. (2002). Symbolically speaking: A connectionist model of sentence production. *Cognitive Science, 26,* 609–651.

Chang, F. (2009). Learning to order words: A connectionist model of heavy NP shift and accessibility effects in Japanese and English. *Journal of Memory and Language, 61,* 374–397.

Chang, F., Bock, K., & Goldberg, A. E. (2003). Can thematic roles leave traces of their places? *Cognition, 90,* 29–49.

Chang, F., Dell, G. S., Bock, J. K., & Griffin, Z. (2000). Structural priming as implicit learning: Comparison of models of sentence production. *Journal of Psycholinguistic Research, 29,* 217–229.

Chang, F., Dell, G. S., & Bock, J. K. (2006). Becoming syntactic. *Psychological Review, 113,* 234–272.

Chang, F., Janciauskas, M., & Fitz, H. (2012). Language adaptation and learning: Getting explicit about implicit learning. *Language and Linguistics Compass, 6,* 259–278.

Chen, B., Jia, Y., Wang, Z., Dunlap, S., & Shin, J. A. (2013). Is word-order similarity necessary for cross-linguistic structural priming? *Second Language Research, 29,* 375–389.

Chen, X., Hartsuiker, R. J., Muylle, M., Slim, M. S., & Chi Zhang, C. (2022). The effect of animacy on structural Priming: A replication of Bock, Loebell and Morey (1992). *Journal of Memory and Language, 127,* article 104354. https://doi.org/10.1016/j.jml.2022.104354.

Chomsky, N. (1957). *Syntactic structures.* The Hague: Mouton.

Chomsky, N. (1965). *Aspects of the theory of syntax.* Cambridge, MA: MIT Press.

Cleland, A. A., & Pickering, M. J. (2003). The use of lexical and syntactic information in language production: Evidence from the priming of noun-phrase structure. *Journal of Memory and Language, 49,* 214–230.

Cohen, N. J., & Squire, L. R. (1980). Preserved learning and retention of pattern-analyzing skill in amnesia: Dissociation of knowing how and knowing that. *Science, 210,* 207–210.

Costa, A., Caramazza, A., & Sebastian-Galles, N. (2000). The cognate facilitation effect: Implications for models of lexical access. *Journal of Experimental Psychology: Learning, Memory, and Cognition, 26*, 1283–1296.

Coyle, J. M., & Kaschak, M. P. (2008). Patterns of experience with verbs affect long-term cumulative structural priming. *Psychonomic Bulletin and Review, 15*, 967–970.

De Bot, K. (1992). A bilingual production model: Levelt's "speaking" model adapted. *Applied Linguistics, 13*, 1–24.

Deen, K. (2011). The acquisition of the passive. In J. de Villiers & T. Roeper (Eds.), *Handbook of generative approaches to language acquisition* (pp. 155–188). Amsterdam: John Benjamins.

Dell, G. S. (1986). A spreading-activation theory in sentence production. *Psychological Review, 93*, 283–321.

Dell, G. S., & Chang, F. (2014). The P-chain: Relating sentence production and its disorders to comprehension and acquisition. *Philosophical Transactions of the Royal Society B: Biological Sciences, 369*, article 20120394.

Dell, G. S., Oppenheim, G. M., & Kittredge, A. K. (2008). Saying the right word at the right time: Syntagmatic and paradigmatic interference in sentence production. *Language and Cognitive Processes, 23*, 583–608.

Dell, G., & Reich, P. A. (1981). Stages in sentence production: An analysis of speech error data. *Journal of Verbal Learning and Verbal Behavior, 20*, 611–629.

Dell, G. S., Schwartz, M. F., Martin, N., Saffran, E. M., & Gagnon, D. A. (1997). Lexical access in aphasic and nonaphasic speakers. *Psychological Review, 104*, 801–838.

Desmet, T., & Declercq, M. (2006). Cross-lingustic priming of syntactic hierarchical configuration information. *Journal of Memory and Language, 54*, 610–632.

Dowty, D. (1989). On the semantic content of the notion "thematic role." In G. Chierchia, B. H. Partee, & R. Turner (Eds.), *Properties, types, and meaning* (pp. 69–129). Dordrecht: Kluwer.

Dowty, D. (1991). Thematic proto-roles and argument selection. *Language, 67*, 547–619.

Estival, D. (1985). Syntactic priming of the passive in English. *Text, 5*, 7–21.

Facipieri, C., Vann, M., & Bencini, G. M. L. (2022). Shared syntactic representations in non-native languages. In *Proceedings of the 13th International Conference of Experimental Linguistics* (pp. 57–60). Athens: ExLing Society.

Ferreira, V. S., & Bock, J. K. (2006). The functions of structural priming. *Language and Cognitive Processes, 21*, 1011–1029.

Ferreira, V. S., Morgan, A., & Slevc, R. L. (2018). Grammatical encoding. In S. A. Rueschemeyer & G. M. Gaskell (Eds.), *The Oxford handbook of psycholinguistics*, 2nd ed. (pp. 432–457). Oxford: Oxford University Press.

Ferreira, V. S., and Slevc, L. R. (2007). Grammatical encoding. In M. G. Gaskell (Ed.), *The Oxford handbook of psycholinguistics* (pp. 453–470). Oxford: Oxford University Press.

Ferreira, V. S., Bock, K., Wilson, M. P., and Cohen, N. J. (2008). Memory for syntax despite amnesia. *Psychological Science, 19*, 940–946.

Fillmore, C. J. (1968). The case for Case. In E. Bach & R. T. Harms (Eds.), *Universals in linguistic theory* (pp. 1–88). New York: Holt, Rinehart, and Winston.

Fillmore, C. J. (1985). Frames and the semantics of understanding. *Quaderni di Semantica, 6*, 222–254.

Fisher, C. (2002). The role of abstract syntactic knowledge in language acquisition: A reply to Tomasello (2000). *Cognition, 82*, 259–278.

Fisher, C., Kyong-sun, J., & Scott, R. (2020). The developmental origins of syntactic bootstrapping. *Trends in Cognitive Science, 12*, 48–77.

Fisher, C., Gertner, Y., Scott, R., & Yuan, S. (2010). Syntactic bootstrapping. *Wiley Interdisciplinary Reviews: Cognitive Science, 1*, 143–149.

Flett, S., Branigan, H. P., & Pickering, M. J. (2013). Are non-native structural preferences affected by native language preferences? *Bilingualism: Language and Cognition, 16*, 751–760.

Foltz, A., Knopf, K., Jonas, K., Jaecks, P., & Stenneken, P. (2020). Evidence for robust abstract syntactic representations in production before age three. *First Language, 41*, 3–20.

Foltz, A., Thiele, K., Kahsnitz, D., & Stenneken, P. (2015). Children's syntactic-priming magnitude: lexical factors and participant characteristics. *Journal of Child Language, 42*, 932–945.

Fox, D., & Grodzinsky, Y. (1998). Children's passive: A view from the by-phrase. *Linguistic Inquiry, 29*, 311–332.

Fromkin, V. A. (1973a). Appendix. In V. A. Fromkin (Ed.), *Speech Errors as Linguistic Evidence* (pp. 243–269). The Hague: Mouton.

Fromkin, V. A. (1973b). The non-anomalous nature of anomalous utterances. In V. A. Fromkin (Ed.), *Speech errors as linguistic evidence* (pp. 215–241). The Hague: Mouton.

Gámez, P. B., & Vasilyeva, M. (2020). Shared syntactic representations in balanced bilinguals: Cross-linguistic priming with and without verb overlap. *Language Learning and Development, 16*, 89–106.

Garrett, M. F. (1975). The analysis of sentence production. In G. Bower (Ed.), *The psychology of Learning and Motivation* (vol. 9, pp. 133–177). New York: Academic Press.

Garrett, M. F. (1976). Syntactic processes in sentence production. In R. Wales and E. L. Walker (Eds.), *New approaches to language mechanisms* (pp. 231–256). Amsterdam: North-Holland.

Garrett, M. F. (1980a). Levels of processing in sentence production. In B. Butterworth (Ed.), *Language Production* (vol. 1, pp. 177–220). London: Academic Press.

Garrett, M. F. (1980b). The limits of accommodation: Arguments for independent processing levels in sentence production. In V. A. Fromkin (Ed.), *Errors in linguistic performance: Slips of the tongue, ear, pen and hand* (pp. 263–271). New York: Academic Press.

Garrett, M. F. (1982). Production of speech: Observations from normal and pathological language use. In A. Ellis (Ed.), *Normality and pathology in cognitive functions* (pp. 19–76). London: Academic Press.

Garrett, M. F. (1988). Processes in language production. In F. J. Newmeyer (Ed.), *Linguistics: The Cambridge survey, Ill. Language: Psychological and biological aspects* (pp. 69–96). Cambridge: Cambridge University Press.

Garrod, S., & Anderson, A. (1987). Saying what you mean in dialogue: A study in conceptual and semantic coordination. *Cognition, 27*, 181–218.

Gertner, Y., Fisher, C., & Eisengart, J. (2006). Learning words and rules: Abstract knowledge of word order in early sentence comprehension. *Psychological Science, 17*, 684–691.

Goldberg, A. E. (1995). *Constructions: A construction grammar approach to argument structure*. Chicago: University of Chicago Press.

Goldberg, A. E. (2002). Surface generalizations: An alternative to alternations. *Cognitive Linguistics, 13*, 327–356.

Goldberg, A. E. (2006). *Constructions at work: The nature of generalization in language*. Oxford: Oxford University Press.

Gries, S. T. (2005). Syntactic priming: A corpus-based approach. *Journal of Psycholinguistic Research, 34*, 365–399.

Gries, S. T. (2011). Studying syntactic priming in corpora: Implications of different levels of granularity. In D. Schönefeld (Ed.), *Converging evidence: Methodological and theoretical issues for linguistic research* (pp. 143–165). Amsterdam: John Benjamins.

Gries, S. T., & Koostra, G. (2017). Structural priming within and across languages: A corpus-based perspective. *Bilingualism: Language and Cognition, 20*, 235–250.

Griffin, Z., & Weinstein-Tull, J. (2003). Conceptual structure modulates structural priming in the production of complex sentences. *Journal of Memory and Language, 49*, 537–555.

Griffiths, P. (2006). *An introduction to English semantics and pragmatics.* Edinburgh: Edinburgh University Press.

Grimshaw, J. (1990). *Argument structure.* Cambridge, MA: MIT Press.

Gruber, J. (1965). *Studies in lexical relations.* Doctoral dissertation, MIT, Cambridge, MA.

Hall, M. L., Ferreira, V. S., & Mayberry, R. I. (2015). Syntactic priming in American Sign Language. *PLoS ONE, 10*.

Harley, H. (2003). Possession and the double object construction. In P. Pica (Ed.), *Linguistic variation yearbook* (vol. 2, pp. 31–70). Amsterdam: John Benjamins.

Hartsuiker, R. J., & Bernolet, S. (2017). The development of shared syntax in second language learning. *Bilingualism: Language and Cognition, 20*, 219–234.

Hartsuiker, R. J., Bernolet, S., Schoonbaert, S., Speybroeck, S., & Vanderelst, D. (2008). Syntactic priming persists while the lexical boost decays: Evidence from written and spoken dialogue. *Journal of Memory and Language, 58*, 214–238.

Hartsuiker, R. J., Beerts, S., Loncke, M., Desmet, T., & Bernolet, S. (2016). Cross-linguistic structural priming in multilinguals: Further evidence for shared syntax. *Journal of Memory and Language, 90*, 14–30.

Hartsuiker, R. J., & Pickering, M. J. (2008). Language integration in bilingual sentence production. *Acta Psychologica, 128*, 479–489.

Hartsuiker, R. J., Pickering, M. J., & Veltkamp, E. (2004). Is syntax separate or shared between-languages? Crosslinguistic syntactic priming in Spanish-English bilinguals. *Psychological Science, 15*, 409–414.

Heyselaar, E., Segaert, K., Walvoort, S. J. W., Kessels, R. P. C., & Hagoort, P. (2017). The role of procedural memory in the skill for language: Evidence from syntactic priming in patients with amnesia. *Neuropsychologia, 101*, 97–105.

Heyselaar, E., Wheeldon, L., & Segaert, K. (2021). Structural priming is supported by different components of nondeclarative memory: Evidence from priming across the lifespan. *Journal of Experimental Psychology: Learning, Memory, and Cognition, 47*, 820–837.

Hilpert, M. (2014). *Construction grammar and its application to English.* Edinburgh: Edinburgh University Press.

Hoffmann, T. (2017). Construction grammars. In B. Dancygier (Ed.), *The Cambridge handbook of cognitive linguistics* (pp. 310–329). Cambridge: Cambridge University Press.

Hoffmann, T. (2022). *Construction grammar: The structure of English*. Cambridge: Cambridge University Press.

Hoffmann, T., & Trousdale, G. (Eds.). (2013). *The Oxford handbook of construction grammar*. Oxford: Oxford University Press.

Huttenlocher, J., Vasilyeva, M., & Shimpi, P. (2004). Syntactic priming in young children. *Journal of Memory and Language, 50*, 182–195.

Jackendoff, R. (1972). Semantic interpretation in generative grammar. Cambridge, MA: MIT Press.

Jackendoff, R. (1983). *Semantics and cognition*. Cambridge, MA: MIT Press.

Jackendoff, R. S. (1990). *Semantic structures*. Cambridge, MA: MIT Press.

Jackendoff, R. S. (2002). *Foundations of language*. Oxford: Oxford University Press.

Jackson, C. N. (2018). Second language structural priming: A critical review and directions for future research. *Second Language Research, 34*, 539–552.

Jackson, C. N., & Ruf, H. T. (2017). The priming of word order in second language German. *Applied Psycholinguistics, 38*, 315–345.

Jaeger, T. F., & Snider, N. E. (2013). Alignment as a consequence of expectation adaptation: Syntactic priming is affected by the prime's prediction error given both prior and recent experience. *Cognition, 127*, 57–83.

Kaan, E., & Chun, E. (2018). Priming and adaptation in native speakers and second-language learners. *Bilingualism: Language and Cognition, 21*, 228–242.

Kantola, L., & van Gompel, R. P. (2011). Between- and within-language priming is the same: Evidence for shared bilingual syntactic representations. *Memory and Cognition, 39*, 276–290.

Kaschak, M. P. (2007). Long-term structural priming affects subsequent patterns of language production. *Memory and Cognition, 35*, 925–937.

Kaschak, M. P., & Borreggine, K. L. (2008). Is long-term structural priming affected by patterns of experience with individual verbs? *Journal of Memory and Language, 58*, 862–878.

Kaschak, M. P., Kutta, T. J., & Schatschneider, C. (2011). Long-term cumulative structural priming persists for (at least) one week. *Memory and Cognition, 39*, 381–388.

Kaschak, M. P., Kutta, T. J., & Coyle, J. M. (2014). Long and short term cumulative structural priming effects. *Language and Cognitive Processes, 3798*, 1–23.

Kaschak, M. P., Loney, R. A., & Borreggine, K. L. (2006). Recent experience affects the strength of structural priming. *Cognition, 99*, B73–B82.

Kempen, G., & Hoenkamp, E. (1987). An incremental procedural grammar for sentence formulation. *Cognitive Science, 11*, 201–258.

Kempen, G., & Huijbers, P. (1983). The lexicalization process in sentence production and naming: Indirect election of words. *Cognition, 14*, 185–209.

Khoe, Y. H., Tsoukala, C., Kootstra, G. J., & Frank, S. L. (2021). Is structural priming between different languages a learning effect? Modelling priming as error-driven implicit learning. *Language, Cognition and Neuroscience, 38*(4), 537–557.

Kidd, E. (2012). Implicit statistical learning is directly associated with the acquisition of syntax. *Developmental Psychology, 48*, 171–184.

Kim, Y., & McDonough, K. (2008). Learners' production of passives during syntactic priming activities. *Applied Linguistics, 29*, 149–154.

Kootstra, G. J., & Doedens, W. J. (2016). How multiple sources of experience influence bilingual syntactic choice: Immediate and cumulative cross-language effects of structural priming, verb bias, and language dominance. *Bilingualism: Language and Cognition, 19*, 710–732.

Kootstra, G. J. & Muysken, P. (2017). Cross-linguistic priming in bilinguals: Multidisciplinary perspectives on language processing, acquisition, and change. *Bilingualism: Language and Cognition, 20*, 215–218.

Konopka, A. E., & Bock, K. (2009). Lexical or syntactic control of sentence formulation? Structural generalizations from idiom production. *Cognitive Psychology, 58*, 68–101.

Konopka, A. E., & Meyer, A. S. (2014). Priming sentence planning. *Cognitive Psychology, 73*, 1–40.

Lakoff, G., & Johnson, M. (1980). *Metaphors we live by.* Chicago: University of Chicago Press.

Lakoff, G., & Johnson, M. (1981). *Metaphors we live by.* Chicago: University of Chicago Press.

Lambrecht, K. (1994). *Information structure and sentence form: Topics, focus, and the mental representations of discourse referents.* Cambridge: Cambridge University Press.

Levelt, W. J. (1989). *Speaking: From intention to articulation.* Cambridge, MA: MIT Press.

Levelt, W. J., & Kelter, S. (1982). Surface form and memory in question answering. *Cognitive Psychology, 14*, 78–106.

Levelt, W. J., Roelofs, A., & Meyer, A. S. (1999). A theory of lexical access in speech production. *Behavioral and Brain Sciences, 22*, 1–38.

Levin, B. (1993). *English verb classes and alternations.* Chicago: University of Chicago Press.

Levin, B., & Rappaport Hovav, M. (1995). *Unaccusativity at the syntax–lexical semantics interface.* Cambridge, MA: MIT Press.

Levin, B., & Rappaport Hovav, M. (2005). *Argument realization*. Research Surveys in Linguistics Series. Cambridge: Cambridge University Press.

Litcofsky, K. A., & Van Hell, J. G. (2019). Bi-directional evidence linking sentence production and comprehension: A cross-modality structural priming study. *Frontiers in Psychology, 10*, article 1095.

Loebell, H., & Bock, K. (2003). Structural priming across languages. *Linguistics, 41*, 791–824.

Mahowald, K., James, A., Futrell, R., & Gibson, E. (2016). A meta-analysis of syntactic priming in language production. *Journal of Memory and Language, 91*, 5–27.

Malhotra, G., Pickering, M. J., Branigan, H. P., & Bednar, J. A. (2008). On the persistence of structural priming: Mechanisms of decay and influence of word-forms. In B. C. Love, K. McRae & V. M. Sloutsky (Eds.), *Proceedings of the 30th Annual Conference of the Cognitive Science Society* (pp. 657–662). Austin: Curran Associates.

Marantz, A. (2013). Verbal argument structure: Events and participants. *Lingua, 130*, 152–168.

Messenger, K. (2021). The persistence of priming: Exploring long-lasting syntactic priming effects in children and adults. *Cognitive Science, 45*, article e13005.

Messenger, K., Branigan, H. P., & McLean, J. F. (2011). Evidence for (shared) abstract structure underlying children's short and full passives. *Cognition, 121*, 268–274.

Messenger, K., Branigan, H. P., & McLean, J. F. (2012). Is children's acquisition of the passive a staged process? Evidence from six-and nine-year-olds' production of passives. *Journal of Child Language, 39*, 991–1016.

Messenger, K., Branigan, H. P., McLean, J. F., & Sorace, A. (2012). Is young children's passive syntax semantically constrained? Evidence from syntactic priming. *Journal of Memory and Language, 66*, 568–587.

McKee, C., McDaniel, D., & Garrett, M. C. (2018). Children's performance abilities: Language production. In E. Fernández and H. Smith Cairns (Eds.), *Handbook of psycholinguistics* (pp. 491–515). Oxford: Wiley-Blackwell.

McDonough, K. (2006). Interaction and syntactic priming: English L2 speakers' production of dative constructions. *Studies in Second Language Acquisition, 28*, 179–207.

McDonough, K., & Chaikitmongkol, W. (2010). Collaborative syntactic priming activities and EFL learners' production of wh-questions. *Canadian Modern Language Review-Revue Canadienne Des Langues Vivantes, 66*, 817–842.

McDonough, K., & Mackey, A. (2008). Syntactic priming and ESL question development. *Studies in Second Language Acquisition, 30*, 31–47.

McDonough, K., Trofimovich, P., & Neumann, H. (2015). Eliciting production of L2 target structures through priming activities. *The Canadian Modern Language Review, 71*, 75–95.

Moutsopoulou, K. Pfeuffer, C. Kiesel, A. Yang, Q. & Waszak, F. (2019). How long is long-term priming? Classification and action priming in the scale of days. *Quarterly Journal of Experimental Psychology, 5*, 1183–1199.

Pickering, M. J., & Branigan, H. P. (1998). The representation of verbs: Evidence from syntactic priming in language production. *Journal of Memory and Language, 39*, 633–651.

Pickering, M. J., Branigan, H. P., & McLean, J. F. (2002). Constituent structure is formulated in one stage. *Journal of Memory and Language, 46*, 586–605.

Pickering, M. J., & Ferreira, V. S. (2008). Structural priming: A critical review. *Psychological Bulletin, 134*, 427–59.

Pickering, M. J., & Garrod, S. (2004). Toward a mechanistic psychology of dialogue. *Behavioral and Brain Sciences, 27*, 169–190.

Pickering, M. J., & Garrod, S. (2013). An integrated theory of language production and comprehension. *Behavioral and Brain Sciences, 36*, 329–347.

Pinker, S. (1989). *Learnability and cognition: The acquisition of argument structure*. Cambridge, MA: The MIT Press.

Potter, M. C., & Lombardi, L. (1998). Syntactic priming in immediate recall of sentences. *Journal of Memory and Language, 38*, 265–282.

Pylkkänen, L. (2008). *Introducing arguments*. Cambridge, MA: The MIT Press.

Ramchand, G. (2008). *Verb meaning and the lexicon: A first-phase syntax*. Cambridge: Cambridge University Press.

Rappaport Hovav, M. & Levin, B. (1998). Building verb meanings. In M. Butt and W. Geuder (Eds.), *The Projection of arguments: Lexical and compositional factors* (pp. 97–134). Stanford, CA: CSLI Publications.

Rappaport Hovav, M., & Levin, B. (2008). The English dative alternation: The case for verb sensitivity. *Journal of Linguistics, 44*, 129–167.

Rappaport Hovav, M., & Levin, B. (2011). Lexical conceptual structure. In K. Von Heusinger, C. Maienborn, and P. Portner (Eds.), *Semantics: An international handbook of natural language meaning* (vol. 1, pp. 418–438). Berlin: De Gruyter Mouton.

Reitter, D., Keller, F., & Moore, J. D. (2011). A computational cognitive model of syntactic priming. *Cognitive Science, 35*, 587–637.

Reitter, D., & Moore, J. D. (2014). Alignment and task success in spoken dialogue. *Journal of Memory and Language, 76*, 29–46.

Roelofs, A. (1992). A spreading-activation theory of lemma retrieval in speaking. *Cognition, 42*, 107–142.

Roelofs, A. (1993). Testing a non-decompositional theory of lemma retrieval in speaking: Retrieval of verbs. *Cognition, 47,* 59–87.

Roelofs, A., & Ferreira, V. S. (2019). The architecture of speaking. In P. Hagoort (Ed.), *Human language: From genes and brains to behavior* (pp. 35–50). Cambridge, MA: MIT Press.

Roland, D., & Jurafsky, D. (2002). Verb sense and verb subcategorization probabilities. In P. Merlo & S. Stevenson (Eds.), *The lexical basis of sentence processing: Formal, computational, and experimental issues* (pp. 325–345). Amsterdam: John Benjamins.

Rowland, C. F., Chang, F., Ambridge, B., Pine, J. M., & Lieven, E. V. (2012). The development of abstract syntax: Evidence from structural priming and the lexical boost. *Cognition, 125,* 49–63.

Salamoura, A., & Williams, J. N. (2006). Lexical activation of cross-language syntactic priming. *Bilingualism: Language and Cognition, 9,* 299–307.

Savage, C., Lieven, E., Theakston, A., & Tomasello, M. (2003). Testing the abstractness of children's linguistic representations: Lexical and structural priming of syntactic constructions in young children. *Developmental Science, 6,* 557–567.

Savage, C., Lieven, E., Theakston, A., & Tomasello, M. (2006). Structural priming as implicit learning in language acquisition: The persistence of lexical and structural priming in 4-year-olds. *Language Learning and Development, 2,* 27–49.

Shattuck-Hufnagel, S. (1979). Speech errors as evidence for a serial ordering mechanism in sentence production. In W. E. Cooper & E. C. T. Walker (Eds.), *Sentence processing: Psycholinguistic studies presented to Merrill Garrett* (pp. 295–342). Hillsdale: Erlbaum

Shimpi, P., Gámez, P., Huttenlocher, J., & Vasilyeva, M. (2007). Syntactic priming in 3- and 4-year-old children: Evidence for abstract representations of transitive and dative forms. *Developmental Psychology, 43,* 1334–1346.

Shin, J. A., & Christianson, K. (2009). Syntactic processing in Korean–English bilingual production: Evidence from cross-linguistic syntactic priming. *Cognition, 112,* 175–180.

Shin, J. A., & Christianson, K. (2012). Structural priming and second language learning. *Language Learning, 62,* 931–964.

Schoonbaert, S., Hartsuiker, R. J., & Pickering, M. J. (2007). The representation of lexical and syntactic information in bilinguals: Evidence from syntactic priming. *Journal of Memory and Language, 56,* 153–171.

Slobin, D. (1996). From "thought and language" to "thinking for speaking." In J. Gumperz & S. C. Levinson (Eds.), *Rethinking linguistic relativity.* Cambridge: Cambridge University Press.

Snyder, W. & Hyams, N. (2015). Minimality effects in children's passives. In E. Di Domenico, C. Hamann, & S. Matteini (Eds.), *Structures, strategies and beyond: Essays in honour of Adriana Belletti* (pp. 343–368). Amsterdam: John Benjamins.

Tannen, D. (1989). *Talking voices: Repetition, dialogue and imagery in conversational discourse*. Cambridge: Cambridge University Press.

Tomasello, M. (1992): *First verbs: A case study of early grammatical development*. Cambridge: Cambridge University Press.

Tomasello, M. (2000a). Do young children have adult syntactic competence? *Cognition, 74*, 209–253.

Tomasello, M. (2000b). The item-based nature of children's early syntactic development. *Trends in Cognitive Sciences, 4*, 156–163.

Tomasello, M. 2003: *Constructing a language: A usage-based theory of language acquisition*. Cambridge, MA: Harvard University Press.

Tooley, K. M., & Bock, K. (2014). On the parity of structural persistence in language production and comprehension. *Cognition, 132*, 101–36.

Ungerer, T., & Hartmann, S. (2023). *Constructionist approaches: Past, present, future*. Cambridge: Cambridge University Press.

Valian, V. V. (1986). Syntactic categories in the speech of young children. *Developmental Psychology, 22*, 562–579.

Valian, V. (2009). Abstract linguistic representations and innateness: The development of determiners. In W. D. Lewis, S. Karimi, H. Harley, & S. O. Farrar (Eds.), *Time and again: Theoretical perspectives on formal linguistics in honor of D. Terence Langendoen* (pp. 189–206). Amsterdam: John Benjamins.

Valian, V. V. (2016). When children don't say what they know: Syntax acquisition and executive function. In D. Barner and A. S. Barron (Eds.), *Core knowledge and conceptual change* (pp. 261–276). Oxford: Oxford University Press.

van Gompel, R. P., & Arai, M. (2017). Structural priming in bilinguals. *Bilingualism: Language and Cognition, 21*, 448–455.

Vasilyeva, M., Waterfall, H., Gámez, P. B., & Gómez, L. G. (2010). Cross-linguistic syntactic priming in bilingual children. *Journal of Child Language, 37*, 1047–1064.

Vernice, M., Pickering, M., & Hartsuiker, R. (2012). Thematic emphasis in language production. *Language and Cognitive Processes, 27*, 631–664.

Warren, P. (2013). *Introducing psycholinguistics*, Cambridge: Cambridge University Press.

Weiner, E. J., & Labov, W. (1983). Constraints on the agentless passive. *Journal of Linguistics, 19*, 29–58.

Wheeldon, L. R., & Konopka, A. (2023). *Grammatical encoding for speech production*. Cambridge Elements in Psycholinguistics. Cambridge: Cambridge University Press.

Ziegler, J., Bencini, G., Goldberg, A., & Snedeker, J. (2019). How abstract is syntax? Evidence from structural priming. *Cognition, 193*, article 104045.

Ziegler, J., & Snedeker, J. (2018). How broad are thematic roles? Evidence from structural priming. *Cognition, 179*, 221–240.

Ziegler, J., Snedeker, J., & Wittenberg, E. (2018). Event structures drive semantic structural priming, not thematic roles: Evidence from idioms and light verbs. *Cognitive Science, 42*, 2918–2949.

Zwaan, R. A., & Radvansky, G. A. (1998). Situation models in language comprehension and memory. *Psychological Bulletin, 123*, 162–185.

About the Author

Giulia M. L. Bencini is an Associate Professor of English Language, Translation, and Linguistics at the University of Bologna, Italy. With a background in experimental linguistics and psycholinguistics, her research focuses on developing linguistically sound, processing-compatible theories that explain both language representation and use. She employs structural priming to explore how language is represented and processed in various populations, including children, adults, second language learners, and multilingual individuals.

Cambridge Elements ⚌

Psycholinguistics

Paul Warren
Victoria University of Wellington

Paul Warren is Professor of Linguistics at Victoria University of Wellington, where his teaching and research is in psycholinguistics, phonetics, and laboratory phonology. His publications include *Introducing Psycholinguistics* (2012) and *Uptalk* (2016), both published by CUP. He is a founding member of the Association for Laboratory Phonology, and a member of the Australasian Speech Science Technology Association and the International Phonetic Association. Paul is a member of the editorial boards for *Laboratory Phonology* and the *Journal of the International Phonetic Association*, and for twenty years (2000–2019) served on the editorial board of *Language and Speech*.

Advisory Board

About the Series

This Elements series presents theoretical and empirical studies in the interdisciplinary field of psycholinguistics. Topics include issues in the mental representation and processing of language in production and comprehension, and the relationship of psycholinguistics to other fields of research. Each Element is a high quality and up-to-date scholarly work in a compact, accessible format.

Cambridge Elements ≡

Psycholinguistics

Elements in the Series

A full series listing is available at: www.cambridge.org/EPSL